The Habit Formula

Life's Success Equation

Dr. Stephanie Aldrich

Copyright © 2019 Stephanie Aldrich
All rights reserved.
ISBN-978-0-578-44380-5

Dedication

To my family, Steven and Noah, for being my true loves and the reason I get up in the morning!

To my loving parents, Frank and Debbie, and sister, Heather, thank you for being wonderful examples and always pushing me to be my best! Thank you for never putting limits on my dreams!

To my bestie Amanda, I'm so grateful that you're willing *and* able to get crazy with me. When's our next adventure?

To Dr. Christina Blatchford, thank you for showing me a different way of doing things. This book would not have been possible if I didn't learn new habits!

To my office team, we are working together to build our dream lives. Thank you for working hard every day!

To Peggy McColl, the mentorship you've given me has completely opened my eyes to the endless possibilities of the universe!

To Bob Proctor and Sandy Gallagher, thank you for helping me shift my own paradigms and create my dream life! It's happening!

Endorsements

"An effective skillset formula easy to implement in order to change habits for the better radically." – Callie K LeVina

"Dr. Stephanie Aldrich really practices what she preaches in this amazing book! She had been practicing dentistry for an impressive twenty years when she decided that she wanted to make some changes in her life and dental practice to be able to enjoy both even more. She realized that changing her ways after doing them the same for this long period of time is possible, but it does take both time and energy - and of course, following the steps in this terrific book - anything is possible!"- Christina Blatchford, DMD, Author of *Playing your A Game 2.0*, CEO of Blatchford Solutions

"Dr. Stephanie Aldrich is not only an extremely accomplished dentist, but her various passions are shown in her being a gifted author of several books on many topics. She also has been a great mom to her son and wife to her husband. It has been my pleasure to know Dr. Stephanie and follow her various skills and talents." – Carol Bognar, RDH, private consultant

"I have known you all your life. You have always been very focused, friendly and professional in everything you have done. You have achieved much in life due to your focus, education and values. I wish you continued success in your dental practice and in life. Thank you for being you." – Alan Wilson, CPA

"Dr. Aldrich is one of the smartest, most caring, motivated people I know. Her life is a success story – God, family, friends, and her dental practice. If you could bottle up her drive, energy, ambition, it would be a model for how to live life!" – Michael Shiplett, Ohio Market President Citizen's Bank

"Dr. Stephanie Aldrich is one of the most amazing women I have met. Through our journey together of personal development and entrepreneurship I have found that strength and inspiration come from many sources if you are open to receive it, and let it change your life. *The Habit Formula* is a fantastic book for anyone who needs a little push, and a good recipe to eat on a daily basis in your life. I found so many things that I was lacking or simply procrastinating about and after reading the book I am now challenged and motivated to make those things happen I did have a couple of things that I was already on point with and doing in my daily life which has made a huge difference in how I work and that was getting organized as Dr. Aldrich mentioned. Sometimes baby steps are all we need to see tremendous results in our life. I am sure you find this book of a complete and unique mastery formula of changing your habits that ultimately will change your life and how you approach things in more ways than you can imagine." – Dr. Yvonne Coleman-Burney, Metaphysical Psychologist and Relationship Consultant.

"This book is an easy read. Breaking a lifetime of habits is not so easy. That's what I thought until I read this book. *The Habit Formula* is written in a manner that we can all relate to. It brings forth the fact that our habits have become 'our way of life'.

Changing the negative that we do is made possible with the steps provided. This book isn't just a help-yourself book, it's a guide, a reference book that no matter what assignment you're on, you can and should return to the introduction just like reading a roadmap. You can look back to see where you started and not just where you are today but what your destination ahead will be like. If you don't skip any of the steps, this book will keep you on track." – Donna Raga

"This book is a game changer. I feel like Stephanie knew what was holding me back from making changes in my life. After reading this book it seems so simple. The few changes I have already made have empowered me to make more. This book is a relief if you are feeling trapped in your daily routines." – Sheila Reckner

"Great strategies and tips for anyone who wants to change their habits and improve their lifestyle" – Joy Walraven, R. Ac., R. TCMP, CST

"Change-seekers will find a track to run on with *The Habit Formula*. Personal growth is simplified with the use of manageable daily goals. These goals provide both accountability and a way to measure your success!" – Amanda Silfani

CONTENTS

Dedication ....

Endorsements ....

Preface 1

Introduction 3

Chapter 1 - The Habit Formula 9

Chapter 2 - Awareness 29

Chapter 3 - Decision 51

Chapter 4 - Mentor 61

Chapter 5 - Choices 73

Chapter 6 - Persistence 97

Chapter 7 - Habit Mastery 111

Preface

I grew up in a family that never set any limitations for me. As I got older, I realized the only limitations were ones that I put on myself. Pressures from the outside world, opinions of others, and past experiences can be very strong deterrents to making changes and getting the desired results.

As adults, it seems like making changes are even more difficult. Social pressures, expectations, and cultural habits influence the decisions and actions that are taken. What we need to realize, is that we truly are free to live the life we want to live. It's our choice. To have enough time, money, and energy to spend with the people we love, doing the things that we love.

In 2017, I watched *The Secret* for the second time, and for some reason it resonated with me this time around. I Googled Bob Proctor, and wanted to learn more about the Law of Attraction and how to attract the things I wanted in my own life. I then discovered Dr. Christina Blatchford, who knew of systems that could help me live *my* life, instead of living for my dental practice.

Through Bob Proctor's *Paradigm Shift* seminar, I met Peggy McColl, who helped me with this book and opened a whole new creative world for me. I didn't realize that I enjoyed writing and teaching. Dr. Blatchford focused some of my attention on my dental practice and how to become efficient and effective in managing it. Peggy and Bob helped me focus the rest of my attention in a new direction of teaching and writing.

The Habit Formula came out of this focus. I use this formula every time I want to change something. If I am creating a new goal, I use the questions to help me map out the steps I need to take to get me to the goal. I use my to-do list to take action every day towards my goal. I think this is the golden nugget to this whole process. Nothing happens until you take action. I know it works and I hope that it helps *you* achieve everything *you* want in your life!

Introduction

The Habit Formula was born out of my own experience with "changing my ways." As I hit my 40s, I started to question my decisions in life, and wondering whether I was doing all that I could do.

I think it's called a "midlife crisis."

Whatever it was, I started to evaluate the things I was good and successful at, and things I wasn't good at. This led to some self-awareness. I also came to the conclusion that I needed to change some things if I were to do the things that I wanted for the rest of my life.

Mastery comes into play when a skill becomes ingrained in our personalities or our normal behavior. Doing something over and over again, and having a predictable outcome, is the key to success. If you can take that skill and apply it to every aspect of your life, there's no way success will not follow.

But what does it take to achieve mastery in something?

You need the training or education required to execute the particular skill set, which requires a teacher or mentor. More importantly, you must also *commit* to this new training, and make daily choices that coincide with this training each and every day.

Through repetition and persistence, mastery will follow. This is the crux of *The Habit Formula*! Throughout this book we will explore what habits are and how they run our everyday routines. You will learn not only *how* to shatter the habits holding you hostage, but *use* the good habits that define you and your personality to help you become the person you want to be.

All habits are a form of social influence. Our beliefs, attitudes, and behaviors are ultimately controlled by the repetition of our surroundings. The people we live around, our environment, cultural customs, and our own experiences in life influence the patterns of behavior that develop into our daily and characteristic habits. The simple way to do this is through repeating those good habits and becoming a master.

Throughout this book, we're going to be looking at how habits control your life, where they come from, and how to break them down to create a new habit that will snowball your actions to leading the kind of life that you want.

It truly is a very simple formula that, if done consistently, will completely change your life for good! Once you master the formula, you will just wash and repeat. By repeating these habits, you will keep doing them without even thinking about them. This will allow your mind to focus on other areas of your life that you want to change and improve.

I wrote this book to make your life easier. Why complicate things?

We have choices in everything we do each and every day. These choices lead to patterns of behavior that lead to our usual habits. These habits then lead to our results. When you make a decision to change your choices, you will ultimately make the decision to change your results, *and* your life!

This is just how things work!

I'm not in my 20s anymore. Ah, the 20s– – when nothing is set in stone. You are free to explore the world and yourself, decide who you are, who you want to spend time with, and how you want to live.

This freedom we have in our youth can form powerful habits, good and bad, that we tend to have for the rest of our lives. Only with experience with these habits, and self-observation can we change the bad ones and keep the ones that work for us.

I'm not much of a reader unless it has to do with business and issues with my industry, but lately I've started reading about why we do the things we do, and it led me to write this book about habits.

You may not realize it, but habits do control our lives!

Everything we do is from some learned set of behaviors that get us a certain result. This made me think in my own life. How can I change *my* habits to get the results that *I* want?

I've been a general dentist, owning my own practice since 2000. I love practicing dentistry but I don't love a lot of the things that go along with it. I figured the easiest way to get where I wanted to go was to find someone who was doing things differently, and just do what they're doing. Don't reinvent the wheel. Sounds simple enough. And you know what? I'm doing just that.

I found a dental consultant who not only made more money than I was making, but also worked fewer hours. My curiosity got the best of me. Or maybe I just was tired of working all the time, not taking any fun vacations with my family, and finally made the decision to change. I hired my consultant. After implementing a few major changes, I'm now making more money than I ever have, *and* do it in less time.

Being free from the office has given me time to spend on myself. What do I want to do with that free time? I love helping people; that's why I got into dentistry in the first place. But I only help a few thousand people a year in my community.

How can I help *more* people and use my psychology background, I wondered. Writing this book and all the other books and programs on this and different subjects will do just that. For some reason, I can find a problem and then find a simple solution to that problem. Sometimes it's from experience, knowing what works and what doesn't work. Sometimes it's from doing it another person's way to get their results.

I would like to be your habit coach – your simplicity consultant who will help you reach your goals and get the results you want in your life. This book is your starting point to do just that. I want to break down why you have the habits that you do, what things need to change in order to develop different habits, and how to change them step by step.

The formula is laid out for you chapter by chapter. All you have to do is follow the exercises after each chapter and figure out what habits you want to change and then take action! It's not a difficult thing to do. Doing it every day is the most difficult part, but if you truly want to change, you will do everything you can to do it.

It won't take a lot of time every day, but it may take some time overall to achieve your goal you have in mind. That's okay

– just nibble at it every day and before you know it, you'll be doing something completely different in life!

It sounds very labor intensive, but I assure you it's not. The faster and simpler you do this, the more confident you'll get at handling any obstacle or bad pattern that develop and get in your way.

I have been practicing dentistry for almost 19 years. I have learned to do things efficiently and effectively and my patients respect that. No one likes going to the dentist; I know this. But if I can do things quickly, less costly, and with as little pain as possible, why wouldn't you be my patient? I have certain habits that I perform every day with every patient. This leads to predictable results and patients being amazed that I am done with their procedure and they can go enjoy the rest of their day.

What set of habitual patterns do you have? Are they working for you or against you?

In this book we will explore what habits are, how we use our habits in our daily lives, and how to change the ones that aren't giving us the results that we want. You have to trust me. You have to put blind faith in a total stranger to help you with your life. My own track record speaks for itself and I am continually improving the bad habits that I possess each and every day.

I want to simplify things for you. I want to give you the habit mastery formula. If you don't care about the explanation of habits and why we do what we do, and just want to get started changing things in your life, skip to Chapter 5. Here you will find easy step-by-step instructions on how to do just that: how to become the master of *your* habits. You can always come back and read the background information, but if you want to get started right away, go ahead to Chapter 5. You're not hurting my feelings!

I want you to take action and if you're anything like me, you're probably already an action person, but don't know *how* to do this. Chapter 5 will lay it out for you. If you want me to go even further in depth into your habits and the steps you need to take to change them, or maybe need me to hold your hand and nudge you a bit, I also have developed programs that accompany this book to create simple action steps that you will do every day until your results are met.

Then you can pick something else to work on and repeat the steps. I'm basically showing you how to fish so you can repeat the steps. You can always change a pattern or behavior that is not getting you the results you want.

Go to www.thehabitformula.com and sign up for one of the programs! It will propel you into your new life faster and easier than you've ever thought possible!

Chapter 1
The Habit Formula

A + D + M + C + P= HM

The formula consists of five parts:

1. Awareness
2. Decision
3. Mentorship
4. Choices
5. Persistence

These five parts added together results in HM or habit mastery. None of the parts can be left out, and they can't be done out of order because one leads into the other.

So, let's start from the beginning.

What are habits? According to Dictionary.com, habits are "an acquired behavior pattern regularly followed until it has become almost involuntary." This means that we learn these behaviors during our lives, and then we repeat them so many times that they become our norm – so normal to us that we don't even think about doing that particular behavior. We just automatically act in that same way when that same circumstance presents itself.

Hmm. If a negative behavior can become automatic and an involuntary part of our life, then either we must make the behavior different, or not follow it regularly, so that we're conscious of this particular behavior pattern and we can change it to get the results we want.

Okay, easy enough, right? A big challenge to all of this is the awareness or realization that we are in a pattern of behaviors to begin with. So, what are our habits?

Let's start with our morning routines. This set of habits start our day and can lead us down the path to how the rest of the day will go. Are you the first one up? Do you get ready, shower, do your hair or make-up, and so on before waking everyone else up? Do you start the coffee machine and pack lunches before the kids come down? Or do you get everyone up at the same time, get the kids dressed and fed and out the door to wait for the bus, and then concentrate on yourself?

Well, these are two examples of morning routines. Neither is right or wrong, but they are very different. If one thing is off, would it set off a chain of disruption that could spoil the whole morning? Sure. What if a kid is sick? What if your alarm didn't go off on time? Would you do things differently to try to get everyone out on time?

What would you do differently? Maybe have a fast and easy breakfast. Or you could give the kids money so that they could buy their lunch instead of you making it.

If there are things that you would do differently in the above scenario with a glitch in a simple morning routine, then why wouldn't we try to make this more efficient right from the start?

It's because of habits.

We repeat the same actions day after day after day, and in the same way, until we don't think about it anymore. We just do them in the same way, and in the same order, because we know we'll get the same results *if* we do it that way.

Why?

We need to realize that this morning "habitual" routine is not the *only* way of doing it. Many families have two parents or a parent and grandparent that help divide and conquer the morning routine successfully. Some families have the kids themselves get ready for school because the parents leave for work before the kids are awake.

Does this make them wrong? No, of course not! They are just different. Some are better than others. While some are more ideal, all of them work to get to their endpoint.

If our morning habitual patterns change for more than one day, like if a child was sick for a few days or if a parent's work schedule changed, will we go back to our old way of doing things, or will we continue to behave in the new way, making the new way our new norm?

I think it depends on how easy the change was and if the successful endpoint was reached. I also think that it depends on whether the change was necessary in the long term, or just a minor disruption. What if the older sibling helped get the younger one ready for school and allowed you enough time to get ready before the kids left for school?

Would you continue this pattern after your sick child was better? It would give you less to do and give the older sibling more responsibility. It would allow you time to do something else in the morning. It seems logical to follow the new pattern of behavior, doesn't it? We all know that humans are never 100% logical; if we were, the world we live in would be much, much different.

Sometimes we must change our behavior patterns because of circumstances, like a new job schedule. Why should we allow outside circumstances to make us find solutions to situations that our habits solve?

This is a great question, and one we will explore many times throughout this book. If we can become *aware* of what our habits are, what our habits *should* be, and *how* we can change them, this can result in our success in anything we want: our health, our income, or our relationships.

It's our regular behavior patterns that, over time, dictate the outcome of our lives.

That's a big statement!

If we can change the behavior patterns that sabotage our outcomes, then we should be able to change the things we want to change in our lives! Some of these things can be so small, but if we tweak them just a little, they can steer us into a totally different path.

It's like a fork in the road. If you go left, at first, you're still close to the right path. But soon you find yourself in a completely different area of town, nowhere close to the right path.

A small change in a habitual pattern can have the same effect on your life. At first you think it's small, but this pattern may influence other patterns in your life, and can become a huge change over time. At some point, you can look back at this small tweak, and realize how important it became to your results.

We have to take a look at where we get our habits in the first place?

We learn these behavior patterns from other people. If we learn our normal habits from other people, why can't we learn new patterns from someone else? Someone who gets the results that we want? Someone who makes more money than we do? Someone who has a clean house? Someone who has a loving relationship? Someone who is healthy and full of energy?

Maybe we're just not *aware* that we can learn different behavior patterns that become regular habits. Or – the bigger observation – maybe we don't *want* to change.

If you're reading this book, I'm led to think that you want to explore your behavior patterns, and learn different ways to improve them, so you can develop the habits necessary to obtain the results that you want. If not, you'd be happy and go along with whatever happens in your life. But you're here with me. So, let's explore more on the habits that rule our lives.

Another definition of habits from Dictionary.com is "a customary practice or use."

Eating is a customary practice that we do every day. But not everyone eats in the same way. There are thousands of "diets" or eating patterns out there, but everyone's body break down the foods they eat differently, so one way of eating may not work for everyone.

In my mid-40s, what I call my "fatties" decade, I've discovered that the eating habits I enjoyed throughout my life were catching up with me. No matter how much I worked out, my body wasn't responding. In fact, it was going the other way, and I was starting to gain the pounds, especially on my mid-section.

I didn't like it, so I decided to look into a different way of eating. I had recently viewed a PBS special on eating high-fat, low-carb foods. I was skeptical at first, because this went against everything I knew from the past. After doing more research on the internet, I knew it wouldn't be difficult, and I decided to give it a try. I figured my old way of eating wasn't doing me any good, so why not eat a new way?

Since you don't know me very well, I usually don't give anything a try. I usually go balls-to-the-wall and quickly turn the switch on and off immediately. I did this with this new diet. I told my hubby, who also wanted to drop some weight, that we were going to eat differently, and to be patient with it to see what happened. Within a month of eating on the ketogenic diet, we both started losing weight. As I'm writing this book, about nine months after switching gears with our eating habits, we've lost a combined 80 pounds! Remarkable!

We don't even kill ourselves with working out either. I do Tae Kwon Do 2 or 3 times a week and that's it! My hubby has a physical job inspecting homes and that's all the physical activity he does.

I love to cook, so learning new recipes with new and different ingredients has been fun and exciting to me. My hubby is loving it too! He's so excited when he starts smelling something coming from the kitchen. He knows it's going to taste good, and it will also help him lose weight!

I'm not saying that this diet or eating pattern is for everyone, and that you should jump into it. I'm not a doctor, and your health concerns may not indicate that this diet will work for you. But what I am saying is that if you want to be healthier, to lose weight, to feel better in your own skin, you first need to decide what size you want to be, and then see your doctor and decide what eating patterns will work best for you and your body type. Then go on the internet and find yummy recipes that you can enjoy, but also make your body work *for* you, not *against* you!

If you hate cooking or don't know how to cook, find out which foods will benefit you. Make sure that they are prepared in the way that benefits you, and then get on your local restaurants' websites, and find foods that you can eat. Then, go there on a consistent basis and eat these foods!

It's very simple: don't complicate things.

I think this is what gets in people's way about changing their habitual patterns. They either overthink it, or they make it so darn complicated that they never do it. Don't over-complicate anything! Life is as simple as you make it! Follow the formula!

If you want to lose weight, find recipes or restaurants that have the food that you need to eat to accomplish your task, and then eat that food. Simple!

It's all about how you see things. It's your perception on the matter, which is also a habit that we'll talk about later in this book.

Everyone *knows* that what you put in your body directly affects how your body reacts and works. But not everyone knows what *types* of foods or supplements they need to make their bodies work efficiently. Science is always changing and learning how our bodies function. There are so many diets out there that it can be confusing.

Let's look at the Mediterranean diet, for example. People in this area of the world eat mostly fresh fish, lean meats, whole fruits and veggies, and whole grains and oils.

Why do these people eat this way?

Because they live by an ocean where fresh fish is abundant. They have lush countrysides where they can grow fruits and veggies, and olives for olive oil. But they also have a habit of walking everywhere.

Most cities in Greece and Italy have small winding streets, some curving around mountain sides where cars cannot go. They control their portion sizes, and eat their grains, pastas, and breads as part of their meals. They don't make them the main portion of their meal. Their eating habits have thus developed into certain patterns over time. They mostly eat whole, unprocessed foods, and get regular exercise. Hmm. Makes sense, right?

This is totally the opposite from the French, whose eating habits consist of heavy cream sauces and pastries with a lot of butter. They love their cheeses, breads, and of course, their wine.

One thing that is noticeable is that they don't eat as much sugar as what other countries consume. It's a fact that higher fat foods not only break down slower in the body than sugary foods, but they also fill you up faster, decreasing your urges for that high carb snack in the middle of the afternoon.

This is what I have found being on the ketogenic diet. I eat one big meal a day, usually lunch, and then I may have something small for dinner or nothing at all. I'm just not hungry!

These are two extremes of eating habits that still work. Neither one is better than the other. They both work for maintaining a healthy lifestyle. They both form a habit of eating freshly prepared food, and shy away from processed items.

I know that most women in the United States have a job and/or are responsible for the grocery shopping and meal preparation. This makes *us* responsible for our families' eating habits. If we are healthy, it's more than likely our families will be healthy too.

Later in this book, we'll specifically talk about our health, and find ways to change our habits, making them involuntary, so we don't even think about them anymore.

We'll find steps that will seem foreign at first, but after some time will become our new norm. We must explore different ways of doing things if we want a change or a certain outcome to occur. The rest will work itself out in the end.

Another definition of a habit from Dictionary.com is "a dominant or regular disposition or tendency; prevailing character or quality." Let's look at always being late as a habit. Why would one person always be on time, or even early for an event, while another person is always late? What does the early person do differently than the late person to come up with different results?

Maybe the early person has a habit of impatience? Maybe this person wants to get things done quickly so they can move onto another task that they want to accomplish? Maybe the early person has a habitual attitude that they doesn't want to affect another person's day, or time by being late? Maybe they respect their time and feel that time is important and shouldn't be wasted?

But why? Why do they care about being on time for an event? Were their parents habitually late for everything, making this person miss out on things? Maybe they believe that a set time is a commitment, and they are holding up their end of the commitment.

So, the next question would be:

Why doesn't the late person feel the same way? What habits do they have that are different from the early person? Do they not care? Do they not plan their activities well enough during the day that they can be at the event on time? Do they get involved with too many activities too close to the event time, not allowing enough time to get ready, and arrive on time to the event? Or maybe they are not *aware* that their late arrival delays the start of activities, and disrupts other people's intentions for the event.

I know – there's so much to think about concerning one small habitual behavior that one may have. Some people may *think* it's small while others *think* it's a big deal. I am a practicing dentist. I have my day mapped out in 15-minute increments. If I am late, or a patient is late, that can throw off the other 40 people that I will see that particular day. And if they're late, maybe their kids will be late for their soccer game, or maybe they will be late for an important business meeting.

I pride myself on being on time, or even early, every day. I think it makes the day go smoother, and it also frees up my mind to think about other issues that go on in the office.

I don't have to think about it, being on time is my regular tendency, or my habit. I am on time. I know how long a procedure will take, and I schedule things appropriately. I don't have to rush anything. Now, I'm not saying that *every* day is perfect, but nine times out of ten, they are.

I don't want you to think you have to be *perfect* in your journey to evaluate your habits. No one is. *What I want* you to think about is how can you *improve* your results?

If you work on changing your behavior patterns and your regular tendencies, your results will certainly begin to change. I'm not saying you must be a size-two supermodel. I know I never will be, nor do I want to do what it takes to become one. I do know that I'm very happy with my new and improved body. I feel good, and others are inspired by *my* habits that they want to change theirs too, so they can get their *own* results.

This is what I want from you at the end of this book: to realize that if you just tweak your habits — some a little, and some a lot — you can make a huge difference to your life. I want you to realize that you can have anything you want in your life, big or small. You must first be *aware* that your habits control your results, and you must *decide* that you want to change them in order to change your endpoint.

Another thing to think about is that habits take time to develop. You must become aware of the consequences of your habits, and how they're affecting your life. It's going to take some time to change them.

This is what mastery is all about. Working through the exercises in this book to learn, and practice the skills that are needed to confidently change behaviors and thoughts that lead to different results. Once you master this in one area of your life, you can start using it in others.

Some people will be quicker at it then others because they persist while others do not. "Oh, I don't feel like going to the gym today, I'm too tired. I'll go tomorrow." "I don't want to make those extra three phone calls today, I've had a difficult day, I'll do it later." "Bill always has things come to him easier than I do, I will just let Bill have it."

All of these things are the way you believe, or perceive them to be. Nothing else.

I recently earned my second-degree black belt in Tae Kwon Do. Now I'm not a natural athlete, especially now that I'm in my mid-40s. I certainly never thought I'd go that far in my marital arts studies, especially with my previous sports injuries, and my lack of ballerina-like grace.

All I did was go to class two or three days a week for 45 minutes at a time, and in less than four years later, I became a second-degree black belt. I went to class and the masters taught me different techniques of self-defense and fighting, and I just followed their methods.

I'm not the best at it, but I show up every time with enthusiasm and an open mind. There are a lot of people that attend the same classes that have less money than I do. Some are younger, fitter, and certainly are better martial artists than I. However, I don't go to the classes to compete with them – I go to classes to compete with myself.

I go to learn, to grow, and to get better. I leave my ego at the door. Most of my teachers are younger than I am, but that doesn't mean I can't learn something from them. Every class they give me skills to practice, and I just do them. It seems like, over time, I've just gotten better.

Bruce Lee said he never feared a person that practiced 10,000 kicks one time. He feared the person that practiced 1 kick 10,000 times.

I'm going to get you to start practicing your new habits and skills so many times that you will just automatically do them without even batting an eyelash. It will become second nature to you.

You must accept that developing a new habit or behavior pattern will take time. Be patient. Leave your ego at the door. If you were an expert, you'd already be doing it, and succeeding at what you want.

There are so many things that you already succeed at, so take comfort in that! Open your mind to other methods and ways of doing things, and you'll be surprised at how your life will change.

I also take Tae Kwon Do with my son. When he was three years old, we started going to class together. I wanted to do something together so that we could grow together and have something in common with one another. I wanted him to see that you can do anything you want to do without fear of failing.

You just have to put in the effort, and it will come. Follow the steps that have been laid out before you. It's not brain surgery here. You're unlearning a set of behaviors that have gotten you nowhere, and are willing to learn some new actions and ways of doing something that will change your results down the road.

It took me four years of school after college to learn how to be a general dentist. I laugh now, after doing it for over 19 years, that you graduate being just smart enough not be dangerous.

With practice and repetition, you can learn anything. That's why they call it having a dental "practice." I practice my craft every day. I learn something new every day. It's usually not as big of an idea after 19 years of seeing most things, but I always look for new and better ways of doing something. The older I get, the more I know that I don't know everything, and learning new things gets me excited about my life.

I love to learn new things! Cooking, traveling, and meeting new people are exciting adventures to me. I love to learn new languages and new technology. In this stage of my life, I am learning more about my own mind, and how I can control my thoughts and manifest what I truly want in my life: all things that I will be sharing with you throughout this book.

Be the best you can be!

You can too! You can get different and better results in your life, simply by making different daily choices. You must drop the ego at the door of this change, along with your self-doubt, your failures, and your past experiences. Leave it at the door, and decide to do something different with your life.

Find someone new to share it with. Move to another city, and take that new job that you've always wanted. Don't let anything, or anyone stop you. Push yourself. Push your limits on what you know how to do. Make more sales calls. Help more customers. It's all up to you to put in the work to up the game.

Find someone that knows how to do your new skill or way of life, and learn from them. Do exactly what they tell you, and you will learn that new skill, and experience that new life.

I want this book to be encouragement for you. I'm from a small town in Ohio. I graduated with 44 people in my class. I've been asked how I've been so successful in my life, and I said that I was one of the only people in my class that could read! This isn't a true statement: there are a lot of successful people who were in my class, but there are a lot of them that aren't and never will be.

Why? We all came from the same country town. We had the same teachers. Why did some of us succeed, while others didn't? It all lies in what we did with the basic skills that we were taught in school.

Almost everyone was in a sport. We learned not only the skills to play that sport, but we learned life skills as well:

Be on time.

Eat healthy and don't smoke or drink.

Perseverance.

Be creative.

Make quick decisions.

Repeat actions until they become habits.

Have a strong will.

Enforce your mind over your body.

Work as a team.

Build comradery.

I think that the reason some of us moved onto success in life, is that we kept practicing these life skills *after* school. We used these life skills in different areas of our lives, and allowed them to shape the decisions and choices we made every day. Others forgot about them, and let their present circumstances dictate their lives. Whether it was their lack of knowledge or environment, something held them back, and kept them in the same place that they started.

I don't want the same thing to happen to you. My dental practice plateaued for 10 years. I made the same amount of money for 10 years. It was easy after the second year because we developed daily habits that allowed us to make the same amount of money every year. I already knew how to do it.

Once I wasn't distracted by my young son and my new husband, I started to focus on how I could improve myself, and offer new services to my patients. When I started learning new skills and techniques, and coupled that with new ways to schedule procedures, my income increased.

The change was gradual, but it's such a day-and-night kind of change that I've decided to never go back to the old way of doing things.

My consultant was so impressed with my changes that she's featuring me in her new book. I've even talked with her about doing a joint venture together to help other dentists do the same thing, and get easier and more dramatic results than they ever imagined.

You must realize by now that it all starts with you. You have to make the decision to change. You have to do the work, and make the different daily choices that will end up getting you different results. It all starts and stops with you.

Are you happy where you are? Who you are? What you've become? How much money you make? What you look like? How you feel? Who you hang around?

If not, why?

Why are you letting your crappy, lazy, skeptical habits control you? No one put you in the cage except yourself. Who cares what your parents think? Who cares what your friends think? Don't give energy into your past experiences where nothing worked out for you, and you just gave up.

Don't give up!

This is your new thing! This will become your old thing too! Don't quit. Keep learning new things. Keep improving yourself.

If you don't have plans for yourself, you'll fit into someone else's plans. And they don't want you to succeed. They don't care about you!

Think about how do you want to live? So far, your way isn't working. If it was, you wouldn't still be reading this book, or coming to my seminars and webinars. Why don't you do it my way? It's worth a shot, huh? What do you have to lose? A few pounds? An old crappy job that you hate anyways? A terrible relationship that's not serving your heart and soul? Those things are worth losing. Learn to live your life on your terms, and you will never regret one day.

Assignment #1

A. List 5 habits that you would like to change, improve, or create if there was plenty of time and money to do so. They can be big or small.

    Example List:

        1. Lose weight/be healthy

        2. Save money

        3. Become organized

        4. Be on time

        5. Get up early

B. List 5 things that are holding you back from making these changes:

    Example List:

        1. Money

        2. Time

3. Family obligations
4. Not knowing how
5. Lack of confidence

C. If you acquired or changed the 5 habits listed in question #1, what would your life look like?

Example List:

1. Lose weight - feel more confident, more energetic. Have the confidence to date again or get that job I'm qualified for.

2. Saving money - debt-free, less pressure to make ends meet, travel more, do more with my family.

3. Becoming organized - less stress, less stuff around that I don't use, cleaner house/desk.

4. Be on time - less anxiety/stress, make more money because I can fit more sales opportunities/meetings into the day.

5. Get up early – work out before work begins, have time to plan my day, organize the kids' stuff, write or educate myself on a new skill or hobby, have some "me" time.

Chapter 2
Awareness

(A)+ D + M + C + P = HM

Step #1 to Habit Mastery= Awareness

What is awareness? Awareness comes from having knowledge or consciousness about something. When you're sleeping, and in that deep non-REM sleep that most of us have every night, your mind is not aware that the world is continuing without you.

The Earth is still moving, there's still oxygen in the air to breathe, your dog is sleeping on the bed beside you, and they can easily get up and move somewhere else. Your sensory functions have basically shut down, causing your conscious mind to also shut down. You're not aware of your surroundings until you get up in the morning.

Have you ever dozed off and fell asleep on a long car ride? Or in a meeting? Your mind suddenly became unaware of your surroundings, and then all of a sudden, a loud noise, or someone nudging your arm, or a bump in the road, caused your senses to wake up, and your body to jump as a reflex response.

Did you know that while you dozed off, you started drooling? Or snoring? Or your head was bobbing forward and backward like one of those bobblehead dolls? Nope. You were totally unaware that any of that was going on. But the world around you still moved forward, constantly changing without your participation.

As we put our daily routines into action, we can also become aware of our behavior patterns that give us our results in our personalities, our careers, our relationships, and our physical bodies. You can do some self-discovery.

Becoming aware of your habits is another eye-opening experience. Why do you do the things that you do every day? Good and bad? Why do you put on your makeup the way that you do? Why do you always go to the gym at 5am instead of going after work?

Why do you put your underwear on, then your pants, then your shirt, instead of putting on your shirt first, then your underwear, then your pants? It's all about habit formation. What you're taught, and what behavior patterns you follow every day, day after day, until you don't think about these patterns consciously any more.

Where and how did we learn these behavior patterns?

Another definition from Dictionary.com that we're going to explore on habits is a "particular practice, custom, or usage." Basically, it's the environment that you're in, that you've grown up in. All of your surroundings, people you know, and people that you spend time with influence your daily behavior patterns more than you want to admit.

Let's take a look at your family. Everyone has a group of family members who helped raise you. Whether you had a family with a mother and father figure or you had a single parent who took care of you, it doesn't matter. All of those people taught you how to live your life. They helped you form your opinions about the world, about other people, and the actions you take during your daily routine.

My dad's father was a mechanic and owned a gas station in town. They were very frugal with their money and their resources. They wore the same type of clothes, but always had all the basics they needed. In their early 60s, they had a chance to sell their gas station, and they took the chance. They had scrimped and saved all their lives and felt that they had enough money saved, so they took their chances and retired early, and moved to Florida out of the cold Ohio weather.

Throughout their retirement years, they spent their time travelling throughout North America by motorhome, flipped houses, and invested the money from the sales of those houses wisely. When they passed away, they left a handsome estate that no one thought they would possess. My grandfather's famous saying was, "Don't live high on the hog." That expression to me meant that I shouldn't live to the extreme and should be practical, and not live too extravagant.

Throughout their lives, they made daily choices that grew into lifetime habits: to live within their means, invest the extra money, and continue to work and make money that would sustain their lifestyle and their travels. They worked so they could have fun! Growing up around them, and seeing how they handled money has helped me form choices and lifetime habits on how to accumulate wealth, and save money for a rainy day. My hubby tells me that I save more money than anyone he has ever known, and I'm okay with that!

I learned another lifetime habit about money from my mom. My mother was a stay-at-home mom and always had envelopes of money. She would save money for different things like school clothes, vacations, or whatever special event may be scheduled. She knew how much she needed, and when she needed it. Every time she got a paycheck, she would put money in these different envelopes, and always had enough money for each of those things or events.

I do the same thing. My friend and financial advisor calls me the "squirrel". She tells me I have nuts over here, and I have nuts over there. To me, it's no big deal because I always have enough money for my activities. I save early and I save often. My weekly choices on payday instruct me to see my progress on my envelope savings, and to keep contributing to each envelope until I reach the goal amount. If I don't have any envelopes to save for, I just put that extra in my general savings account so that account builds too.

I know what you're thinking: you're a rich dentist, and I don't make the kind of money that you make! I do make a comfortable living now, but up until a few years ago, I wasn't making a lot of money. I owed hundreds of thousands of dollars in school loans and buying my two practices.

But no matter what, I always had envelopes and savings methods. I skipped vacations, cable TV, and other material things, and put extra money on my loans so I could get out of debt. And it worked! It was worth 13 years of sacrifice so that I could give my new husband and new child the life that they deserve. It's a life that I'm not stressed out about because I don't have creditors beating down my door. Wouldn't it be nice to have no debt and to not feel the daily pressure of having enough money just to pay your bills? It all starts with daily choices that lead to life-long behavioral patterns.

Saving money, paying off debt, and investing money is just one example of daily choices that lead to good life-long habits. I want to dive into this subject and break it down.

If your goal is to save more money, maybe you want to pay off some credit card debt or your car loan. This may feel like a daunting task, but I assure you: you can only pay off these loans, and you can pay them off sooner than you think.

There are many different philosophies to doing this. You can choose whichever way you want. As long as you make a decision that you're going to do it, it doesn't matter *how* you do it, only that you're moving towards your goal of paying off your debt.

I like to pay off the smallest debt first. Some people say to do it this way, while others say pay off the loan that has the biggest interest rate. There are pros and cons to every decision or strategy out there. It doesn't matter, as long as you start to make choices that lean towards accumulating money, and getting rid of the debt.

I like to pay the smallest off first because I feel like it gives me confidence that I can accomplish it, and this momentum allows me to continue with my debt elimination. One down, one more down, etc. I feel accomplishment when I see something happen quickly. It's like losing weight. If you can just lose a couple of pounds by whatever method you choose, you're more likely to keep going. You've built momentum and you start seeing the results quickly. The same is true with money.

You need to break down a habit of saving money into simple daily choices and actions.

Where does all your money go every paycheck? Do you like drinking Starbucks coffee every day? Do you like to shop for clothes, and dress like a fashionista? Do you go out with your friends and families and entertain a lot? Do you go to the gym regularly?

If you do, you must start with creating a budget. I know, budgets. Yuck! But this is the most important step in creating a different future.

You must know your starting point.

If you have these extra-curricular activities, you must cut something. This doesn't mean you have to cut it out completely or forever. You just need some extra money, so you must think about who you're giving your hard-earned money to, and instead, give it to yourself and your debt.

If you can come up with an extra $200 or more a month and put that on your debt, you will start seeing a compounding snowball effect.

Maybe you can have a garage sale, or get rid of some things that you never use like electronics, clothes, or furniture. You can also put this money onto your debt. If it's a car payment, try to double it every month. I've done this several times. I got rid of cable TV and the gym for a while, and used the extra money to pay off my car two years earlier than originally planned.

You can also get a side job to help pay off your debt. Driving for Uber or Lyft is a flexible job that can help you stack up cash so that you can be financially independent. Every Uber driver that I've had so far has told me that they drive to earn extra money for vacations and to fix their houses.

You need some type of part-time job to help build your confidence that you're working hard towards your debt-free goal. There are so many possibilities, even on the internet, to earn extra money without feeling like all you do is work!

I understand that it is difficult. You're an adult. You want to live the life you want. However, this is only a drop in the bucket to getting new and better results. Forming better habits can help build upon each other, and propel you to an extraordinary life.

A small choice now, like saving the $15 you would spend on going out to lunch today, and just pack your lunch, is a great start. This small daily choice can become a huge important habit that you can carry throughout your life.

The sooner you start, the further ahead you will be. This doesn't mean you can never go out for lunch ever again! This just means until your debt is paid off, you're going to do less of it, and pay off your debt.

Remember when you were a kid? Did your family save money? Were they always telling you, "No, you can't buy that? Money doesn't grow on trees!" More than likely your family was always concerned with money – a lack of – and debt. Thanks to them, this is how you are. You learned your habits from them. But, it's not difficult to change and be different from them.

You just have to make different daily choices. Take baby steps every day, and then as time goes on, you won't even have to think about what choices you should make. You'll be out of debt, you'll have money saved, and you'll never go back into debt because you've changed your thoughts and your behavioral patterns towards money.

Later in the book we'll revisit your past. If you can identify *why* you do the things you do to get the results you get, it's easy to tweak your actions so you'll get a different result. It all comes down to small daily decisions. If you want to get different results, don't let other people's habits dictate what you do. No one is 100% correct all the time.

If your family was terrible with money, you probably are, too. You don't know any better. It's not your fault. But this doesn't mean you have to stay that way. You just have to learn a different way of doing things.

Maybe your mom was a pack rat, and your house looked like a disaster zone. More than likely, yours does too. This is how you grew up, and she gave you *her* bad habits of saving everything she ever bought. This doesn't mean you can't unlearn the bad choices, and relearn something good. There's always a reason why we do the things we do.

Cultural customs can also create behavior patterns that we adhere to. In some parts of the world, their diet consists of mainly vegetables and fruit. Usually this is because of their environment. Maybe their environment doesn't sustain many animals. So, their body types will be different than those of people in the Western nations.

In some cultures, there's little room to house their big populations, so people live in small studio apartments, many of which do not have kitchens. These people would not be in the habit of buying household items that would create clutter simply because they don't have the room to store it. These people also would eat out every meal so they wouldn't have to cook.

In certain cultures, religion is an important structure to their daily habit formation. How they eat and dress, and what their roles in society are, could be dictated by their religion.

In the Amish community, once the children reach a certain age, they are allowed to leave their communities and live elsewhere for a certain amount of time. By doing this, they experience other people's cultural habits. They then can decide for themselves if they would like to go back to the Amish community, or find their own way. I think that's a fair way to approach it. People need to make their *own* choices, and learn to live with them, or choose something different.

But we're not readily exposed to other cultures, or others' opinions on different ways of doing things. We are kind of "stuck" in our own environment, around the same people each and every day.

If you're not an avid reader, you may not know that there are a ton of different ways of doing things. Using YouTube or Google can help you find different opinions and methods to reaching a desired result.

Dr. Stephanie Aldrich

We must become *aware* that our way, the way that we were taught is not the *only* way of doing it.

There are other ways to do things. It doesn't mean that a certain way is good or bad, right or wrong. It just means that it's different. Sometimes doing things differently will still get you the same result, and sometimes it will be totally different. You must become *aware* of the different options out there, and see what kind of results they are getting, and then follow their path.

I think this really boils down to finding the end result that you *want*, and then following the way to get there. "Just follow the yellow brick road, Dorothy." We are in the information age. It's a time in history where billions of people are connected with one another through information that can be accessed in seconds through the internet. How wonderful is that?

If I want to learn a new recipe, click on a link, and I can find it. If I want to fix my bike so I can get in shape and save gas money, I can click on a link and find a YouTube video on how to fix my bike. I didn't want to pay someone to drywall my living room, so I just clicked on a link, and watched a video on how to do it myself.

Being curious and self-sufficient is certainly a behavioral characteristic or habit that can help lead you to the results you want. The whole point of this book is to help simplify things for you. I know, you're busy. You've got kids, or no kids but a demanding job. Or maybe you have kids, a hubby, a dog, *and* a demanding job. No matter your situation, the only way you can get different results is to keep it simple, and to stop doing the same things that get you the same results!

You must find a different path if you want to get to a different place.

Sometimes finding the different path is easy, and sometimes it's not. Sometimes you must be a little creative and think out of your small box that you've lived in your whole life. Get the wheels turning inside your brain. Start thinking, and your path will be built right in front of your eyes. Sometimes you need help building the path by finding someone who's already been there, a mentor, for example.

Now, not every day is ideal. Don't worry — we're all human. Sometimes things get off track. Perhaps our kid's birthday party is this weekend, and we really want that piece of birthday cake. Go ahead. Eat a piece of cake! Enjoy it. Then get back on your eating habits, and make the better choice at the next meal, and you'll find yourself back on track.

If you really want that new pair of shoes because you have a fun party you want to go to, go ahead and get them, and have fun at your party. Just don't do it again for a while until you've saved enough money to pay off your debt, or whatever your goal is.

You still have to live, but you also don't want to fall into the same previous behavioral patterns that aren't resulting in the success that you want. Focus on your goal, and things will start to happen. It's all about concentration, and building a new habit. A new habit that will serve you well. If you're *aware* of the choices you need to make because you really want that promotion, or to be debt-free, or to lose weight, you will find that you'll end up with the results you're trying to achieve.

Why? Because you're focused on the end result, and you're taking your steps towards success.

Religion can also play a big role in forming your habits and the way that you do things. Most major religions believe that the results you get are in direct proportion to the actions you take. This is certainly true.

The more good things you do, the more good things that usually come back to you. But what do you believe when something bad happens to someone good? Do you believe that they must have done something wrong to deserve it? Do you believe that everything happens for a reason, and that this will turn into something good that will make you stronger? Or do you believe things happen, and there's no reason for them, they just are?

There's no right or wrong answer to these questions, just general beliefs that control how people react to certain situations. If you're playing a sport and someone beats you, how do you react? Do you feel mad or ashamed, and give up? Or do you decide that you can improve your skills in such a way that you have a good chance of beating the other person or team in the future? Your belief will dictate what actions you take. You'll either practice harder over the off-season, or you'll start doing another activity.

This is the same thing in life. Your perception, the way you see things, totally dictates what actions you take to improve your life or live status quo. If you think that because you live in a certain place, or you're not as smart as that other person, or you don't have money to do that thing like those other people, then you're right! You'll never get out of your current situation. If this, if that. There will always be things that you can't control. Things that happen, good and bad. So what?

You can control *yourself*, *your* body, and *your* mind. You can improve your skills to get whatever you want. The results are out there for everyone. You just have to take the right steps to get there. You may have to step on the toes of those that you love or those close to you. Especially when they see that you're working hard to change your current circumstances.

It all starts with your beliefs. If you believe you can, then you're right! If you believe you can't, then you're right too!

It's all a mind game. Your body will follow what your mind tells it to. Your soul and spirit can control your mind if you allow it to be free, and do what it feels it should do. I know this might sound like hocus-pocus and magic, but it really does make sense.

If you become *aware* that there are different thoughts, opinions, and ways of doing things, you can then open your mind to those differences. These differences can help to reshape your life.

It's okay if you're wrong. It's okay if you need to change course. Take a step back, and see where you need to go, and then just go there. No one's perfect. No one does everything right the first time. So what? Who cares? Give yourself a break! Changing one's life takes time and redirection.

Don't get in your own way and stop being so hard on yourself. That's your environment talking. Someone around you will tell you negative things. Don't listen to them! Listen to your heart and your mind. Listen to that little voice inside your head. It will tell you what you *really* want, and what you *should* believe.

If it seems easy, it is! It also doesn't mean it won't feel uncomfortable, because it will.

Sometimes it will feel like you're doing something wrong. Sometimes it will take every ounce of your strength to keep going. Other times it will just take time to accomplish things. It's not hard, it's just different. Open you mind, and your body will just start doing the different steps. Push it. Push your thoughts. Believe that you can accomplish it. There will be days you don't want to work on it. That's okay, try to keep the momentum going. Don't let your environment influence you anymore. Control it. Use it to your advantage! Don't allow your past failed experiences create a closed mind.

For example, just because you've tried 100 diets, doesn't mean that no diets work. Maybe the fact that you "tried" them was the reason they didn't work. Most diets control the foods that we eat so we don't have more calories in our bodies then we can burn. Usually when you first start a diet, you're super-focused on the logistics of the diet: what foods to buy and eat, and what exercises to do. The problem is the motivation for starting the diet in the first place. Why did you start? Was it to go to a special event? Did you do it to impress someone that you're trying to date?

Sometimes the motivation isn't strong enough to continue on the diet. Usually when the motivation isn't strong enough, or goes away, like the event that's over, we lose our motivation. We quit. Then we start gaining the weight back because our habits of eating revert back to a previous time.

The motivation to continue has to be strong.

If you become sick, have a heart attack, or find out you have cancer, would this be strong enough motivation for you to change your eating habits? Especially when they can help you live a longer healthier life? I think so.

If you never went out on a date because you were too fat, and no one thought you were attractive, and you really wanted a partner and family to spend your life with, would this be a strong motivation to start and continue a new healthier way of living?

If you were single and had two children to take care of, and the next promotion could allow you to buy a nice house that you've always wanted, would this be a strong motivation to study and learn a new skillset? Do your children deserve to have more?

So what if you're overweight?

So what if you're broke and in debt?

So what if you come from a poor neighborhood?

Your past only develops into your future if you surrender to it. If you allow your past experiences to shape your beliefs, and control your daily choices, then they will control your present *and* your future.

You can start and fail 1000 times. It doesn't matter. As long as you keep going, you will eventually succeed. Get your hands dirty, and do the work. It's not difficult to do if your motivation is strong enough. It'll be the same for you.

Don't let your past dictate your future.

Control your present choices, and choose different things. These different things today will shape your future tomorrow. That's just how it works. The Law of Cause and Effect determines all consequences of your actions. We'll learn about that in the next chapter. The choices you made in your past create your present. If you change your present circumstances, you'll change your future.

Just because you had an awful experience on a plane the last time you flew, doesn't mean that this time will be the same. If you allow your fear of flying to control your life, you will never get to explore a different place or culture. Your life will be closed off from the magnificent things that the world has to offer you.

Just because you've been turned down for 12 jobs in the past few weeks, doesn't mean that you're not going to get the 13th. Don't allow failures to create your future. Negative thoughts usually bring negative actions, which create negative outcomes.

Don't be negative!

Sometimes things don't go right. Sometimes you get stuck. It happens. Just keep believing that you can accomplish your end result. Keep taking daily actions towards your goals, and you will reach them!

Form a different experience.

Form a different belief.

If things couldn't be done like this, no one else would be succeeding either.

It does work!

You *can* be thin.

You *can* have some money in the bank!

You *can* get that new job!

Don't look back if there's negativity back there! Look forward. Keep your head focused on what you really want in your life. Focus on what you want to change, and the things you need to do to change them.

Remember that every cause has an effect. Everything you do today will affect tomorrow and beyond. Believe in yourself, whether this is a new road you're taking, or the same one that you're trying to improve. Believe that you can succeed when no one else thinks you can. They are allowing their *own* social influences, past experiences, and their environment to mold *their* opinions and beliefs that shape *their* lives. If you hold onto the belief that you can go in a new and improving direction, plus make the necessary changes, you will get to your end result. It's just a matter of time.

Sometimes we let our environment and our physical senses convince our brains that something is or isn't. Just because you can't see electrons with your naked eye doesn't mean they don't exist. Just because you can't hear noises with higher frequencies than 20,000 Hz, doesn't mean they don't exist.

There's a whole lot out there that we need to experience, but first, we must break out of our current environment, and explore what the universe has in store for us. This is the only way we can break the shackles that are holding us back. We need to move onward and upward. We need to keep taking steps towards goal obtainment.

We need to stop being afraid.

Fear of failure.

Fear of what others think.

Fear that what we want is impossible to achieve.

Fear of the unknown.

If we knew what was going to happen, it would be a very boring world. If we knew what the end result of an action we took today was going to be, we may not have any memories, or learn our lessons that we can take the next step forward. You need to let go of your fears.

That doesn't mean you shouldn't be safe. That doesn't mean that you can get anything you want even if it hurts other people. All it means is that you need to let go of everything and anything that holds you back from getting what you want out of your life.

Let go of not knowing how. The steps you will follow will be unfolded before you. Just follow the path that someone else has figured out. Let go of your past failures and bad luck.

You can open your own doors of opportunity, however big or small. First, you have to open the door and see what's in front of you. If you don't allow others to influence or control your life, you can follow your own path, and make your life what you want.

If you want to change careers, do it. If you want a loving relationship, get it. If you want to lose weight and have money, take actions towards obtaining those desires.

It all starts and ends with you.

Don't allow learned past beliefs to create your future results. Use your own thoughts and wants to control why you get up in the morning.

If you want to provide a better life for your family, do what's necessary in your own life so your actions will help their lives. No one else will give it to you. You have to do it! That doesn't mean you have to impose your will on others, or steal or cheat to get what you want. There are positive things that you can do to get you out of your slump, no matter how bad it is, and get you on the right path to whatever it is you want.

In Chapter 5, we're going to discuss exactly how you're going to make these changes. This is the most important chapter in this book because it's the action chapter. This is where you're going to put your thoughts and actions down on paper so that it's not in your head anymore. This allows you to begin doing your daily actions that will be focused on your goal. These actions will change the bad habits you've accumulated from your social influences, beliefs, and environment, turning them into newer and more effective habits that will allow you to get what you want.

Dr. Stephanie Aldrich

Assignment #2

A. List 5 distractions in your environment:

Example List:

1. Kids

2. Traffic – live in big city

3. Clutter

4. Other people's activities – soccer games, practices, etc.

5. Chores

B. How could you get rid of those distractions to make more time for you? List 5.

Example List:

1. Use public transportation and use that time to read/listen to podcasts/take a class.

2. Hire a cleaning lady to help with chores.

3. Discuss dividing the daily routine with your partner.

4. Say no.

5. Start a car pool club with other families.

Chapter 3
Decision

A + (D) + M + C + P = HM

Step #2 to Habit Mastery = Decision Making

Making decisions for some people is easy. They go with their gut feeling or instincts, and decide on the course of action. Whether it's good or bad, they just go with it, and change things along the way.

For most of us though, decision-making can be a paralyzing thing. Our fear of failure, hurting someone, or making a wrong decision can stop us from making the changes that we know will give us the results that we truly want in our lives. Every decision that we make comes with a consequence. A decision can cause an effect of something else.

Let's take a look at cause and effect.

The Law of Cause and Effect states that everything is created by a previous action. I think this law is of the utmost importance when it comes to shaping our lives. You make one decision, and it takes you on this path. You take an action over there, and it takes you on another path.

There are always consequences for every action that is taken, whether good or bad.

If we are *aware* of this, we can use it for our own purposes. One of the first things you're going to do is to start looking at an end result that you want, and then identify a habit that's standing in your way to reach that goal. You may think to yourself, "I can't do this; I don't have the time." Or, "I can't do this; I don't have the money!" Or, "I'm not that smart" or "I'm not that ambitious." Reaching your results has everything to do with your perception of it.

Another law that we're going to learn about is the Law of Relativity which states that everything in the world is relative. It's neither good nor bad, easy or hard, nor cheap or expensive. It just is. It's all in how you perceive it.

Your perceptions or beliefs are also a habitual behavior that is formed over time from your environment, cultural customs, close family and friends, and past experiences. Again, we can put the Law of Relativity to good use.

Most people never start to work towards losing weight because they've let themselves get extremely out of shape. They are so overwhelmed with changing it that they just give up before they really get started.

I don't want this to happen to you. This book is here to help you make things simple, just doing a few things a day that are super-focused towards your result. If you give yourself a break, stop being so hard on yourself, and take the steps that you need to create a different habit, you will see a huge change in a short period of time.

Your perception of what you can accomplish will change and broaden your opinions on what you can do!

But every action has a consequence, good or bad. You must first decide on a result that you want to accomplish, and then work backwards to simple daily choices that you will make that coincide with your end result.

It is so easy to do!

Your perception of it is what will either make it or break it. Nothing is impossible. Somethings take more time, energy, and money to accomplish, but nothing is impossible. Be a decision maker. Don't worry that you're going to fail. Don't worry that things didn't work out for you in the past. Don't worry what your family will say about your new goals.

It doesn't matter what they think. This is *your* life and the only way you're going to become a master at changing your life, and doing what you truly want, is to make a decision, and go with it.

You can always tweak it in the future. But if you don't make a decision that you're going to start changing your debilitating habits, the ones that are creating the wall between you and success, then nothing will ever change. Don't think that anything is impossible!

Impossible shouldn't even be a word in our vocabulary. I hate this word! If you think something is impossible, then it is. You will never possess the tenacity it takes to receive it. This doesn't mean that someone else can't do it.

Usually it's just knowing *how* to do something. This is where a mentor is vital to accomplishing your results. Your mentor will help you make a list of actions and a new way of thinking that will help you make different choices that over time form different and better habits.

Why stop before you even get started? If Joe is succeeding at his online business and that's what you want to do, talk to Joe, and take notes. Do exactly what he tells you to do. It's not difficult. He's already doing it, just do what he does because he's already figured it out.

If you're doing something that's never been done before, then finding a mentor is not in your deck of cards. If this is the case, then you *must* make daily choices. Figure out which ones work towards your results, and which ones don't.

You must be aware quickly, and make changes in your choices if you see that you're stuck, or moving in another direction from your result. You must be careful to not form a bad habit that will stop you dead in your tracks.

Another word that I hate is "can't."

Yes, you can – you just don't want to!

No one can make you change. Only *you* can! This is a fact of life. One of my friends asked me how I do all the things that I do every day. "Well, I couldn't do all of that," she said. I told her that if she wanted something, she just has to do it. You can find the time, the energy, *and* the money to do what you want. You *can*! No one is stopping you except you.

Sometimes you allow your previous habits, your environment, family, friends, or your past experiences to mold your ambition level and your persistence. I am from America. My mom's side of the family came to Ohio in the early 1800s and founded the town that we grew up in. Those people left their homes, their surroundings, and their normal way of life to come to Ohio and live their dreams. They didn't allow anything to get in their way and neither should you.

If you want a new job but this new job requires you to go back to college, do it. You can do your schoolwork after your kids go to bed, or when they're watching TV.

You can do things little-by-little until you have the training that you need, and then you can go get that new job. You owe it not only to yourself, but your family.

Don't they deserve to see you succeed?

Don't you want to provide a better life for yourself and your family that this new job could create?

We live in a world of convenience. You can borrow money, find scholarships, and get state grants that will help you succeed. All you have to do is decide what you want, and then make small daily choices towards that goal.

At 44, I decided I wanted to pursue my passion of writing. I rearranged my schedule at work so I would only see patients three days a week. This would give me two days to write and work on programs, and then the weekends I could have fun with my family and friends.

My husband yelled at me, saying that all I ever do is work. Isn't that why I condensed my schedule at my practice – so I could take more time off? I told him that's not why I did it. I don't even *feel* like I'm working when I'm writing. It comes very easily to me, and it fulfills the need I have inside of me to be a teacher, and help more people than just drilling on their teeth.

My writings and programs will ultimately help thousands of people beyond Ohio to break down their bad behaviors and thinking habits that are holding them back from living their passions in their lives. You can find the time, the money, and the end result. What you have to find first is your heart.

What do you love to do?

What kind of person do you want to be?

Do you love being the person who is broke, and always borrowing money from everyone? Do you love being the person who can't sit down in their living room to watch some TV because you've got so much clutter in your house you can't even find any surface to sit down on? Do you love being the person who has trained younger, more educated people to do a job position that you know you could totally do?

The answer, of course, is *no*. Unfortunately, you've been that person for too long. You've let months, years, and decades go by, and have done nothing to change it. It's your fault!

The good news about all of this is that you can change it, and it's not hard. The only thing you have to do is know where your start and end points are, and then commit to taking a few small steps every day towards your end point. You will be so amazed at how easy it is and how fast things will start changing.

Our environment, social circles, and previous experiences all influence our thoughts. If you think you can't, you're right! If you think you can, you definitely will, as long as you take steps every day towards your goal.

Action is the only thing that creates results. Your car may be fast, and have plenty of gas in the tank, but if you don't put in the key, start the engine, and drive the car, it will just sit there.

Your thoughts are your choices.

If you make enough of them on a consistent basis, they will turn into a habit that you don't even think about anymore. You will just do it. You will instinctively follow the same behavior patterns over and over again, and you will get the results you want. If there's something you don't want, you must change your thoughts and choices so that your result over time will be different.

Unfortunately, change is something that takes time. An addict will not get off their drug of choice and stay off it instantly. There are physical, mental, and behavioral patterns that must change and become habitual before they can live a healthy, drug-free life.

That's why they call it a habit. Their thoughts and life choices are made over and over again until they instinctively use the drug. They don't even realize consciously that they're doing it. Their mind and body need it, and they make daily choices to get it.

Why can't you do the same thing but with good behaviors? Repeat, repeat, and repeat it over and over again until you don't even think about it.

Let's say you want to clean up your house. The daily choices must be that when something is used, you must find a home for it, and put it back. If you use it up, the container gets trashed. If you buy something, you must donate or trash something. Ying and yang. Keep things in balance. If you start finding some clutter building up in one of your rooms. Take some time, go through it, find a home for what you want to keep, and then get rid of the rest.

It's that easy!

It may take a little time to go through the clutter, but don't worry; take the time to do it. You will feel so satisfied and proud when you achieve your end result because you know you did it! By achieving one result and building a habit to maintain it, you will then have the confidence to pursue another one. Momentum leads to more victories.

You must start today!

If you are totally enthused by this chapter and want to get started right now with the process, go directly to Chapter 5 and do the exercises. If you think you need more help gaining the strength and momentum to get your end result, you can join one of my programs at www.thehabitformula.com where I walk you step-by-step to your end result! I will hold your hand all the way to victory!

Assignment #3

A. List 5 goals you'd like to accomplish in the next year. Again, they can be big or small.

    Example List:

        1. Organize garage

        2. Lose 20 pounds

        3. Get promotion

        4. Take a vacation

        5. Pay off credit card

B. Prioritize the 5 goals listed in question #1- 1 being the easiest and fastest goal to achieve.

    Example List:

        1. Organize garage

        2. Vacation

3. Lose 20 pounds

4. Pay off credit card

5. Get promotion

Chapter 4
Mentor

A + D +(M)+ C + P = HM

Step #3 to Habit Mastery = Finding a Mentor

The easiest and fastest way to get from Point A to Point B is what? A straight line.

The easiest and fastest way to get from where you are to where you want to go, is to find someone that's already there, like a mentor. Then you don't have to learn the path by yourself, or re-invent the wheel, so to speak.

If you want a promotion at work, for example, look to people at work that have the same job as what you're striving for. What habits do they have? What does the new job position entail versus your current position? What habits are holding you back? Were your parents quiet people, making you very quiet and reserved, but the new job position requires you to do some public speaking or team managing? Does the new job position require you to travel all around the world, but you've never been on a plane before?

Do not let your current surroundings restrain you from making that leap!

What daily choices can you make that would change your current state, and help you make the jump to the next step? These are the choices that you should start to focus all your energy and resources towards. Make them simple, but make them often!

I wanted to consolidate my dental practice to three days a week so I could work on my other businesses. These included writing this book, and consulting other businesses on the other days. I found another dentist whose father started a consulting business and taught her how to do this. I hired her, and told her to show me what to do.

It's taken six months, but every day we schedule our patients differently. We have been successful in not only working three days a week, but also earning more money in those three days.

I've learned the lifetime habit of efficiency. I don't have any downtime when I'm at work. I am constantly bopping from patient to patient all day long. I find that I'm getting so much more done during the day, which means we're helping so many more people!

Learning how to become more efficient at my job, and handling my daily activities, has become a new habit that I don't even think about any more. I make sure that the team schedules my day as full as they can, and I know for a fact, that we will make our production goals, and will work to our potentials.

Being efficient has been one big lesson that I readily learned and accepted. I needed to learn *how* to be efficient, and what I needed to do to make my day busy, but go smoothly at the same time.

Who do you know that's getting the results you want? Let's say Bob has the job position that you want. Introduce yourself to Bob, and offer to take him to lunch. Let him know that you are working for a promotion, and you'd like to know what you have to do to get it. Most people will be glad to help, and also be thankful for a free lunch. Ask Bob what duties the new position entails, what the difference between the positions are, and what can you do to get noticed by the boss so that they pick *you* the next time an opening comes up.

Bob knows the answers because he's already done it. You don't have to reinvent the wheel. Just ask, and follow the path.

Maybe Jessica also has the same job position as Bob. Get another person's opinions, and then do what both of them told you. You will certainly gain powerful insights on what choices you need to make that will develop into the habits and actions that your bosses are looking for.

Why figure it out on your own? Why waste this valuable time? Go to the source of information, and do what they tell you to do. It's that easy. They will have so many opinions that overlap that you will find a clear path to take.

I was told how to schedule my patients in a way that would give me plenty of time with all of them while cutting down on wasted time. I didn't reinvent the wheel; I'm not that smart. If I was, I would have figured it out already after practicing for 20 years. I was smart enough to ask a person who was living the way that I wanted to live, and I started doing the same things that she does each and every day.

Is there a class that you want to take that would give you a new skill and help you earn more money? Take it! What's holding you back? Look at it this way, if you don't take it, you'll end up with the same results that you have right now. If you do take it, have you calculated how far ahead you will be with your new skills set? Even if the class costs money, you could earn 10 times that amount if you put the skills into action.

If you want to lose weight, take gym and yoga classes for that. Just sign up. Hire a personal trainer that has not only studied the body and nutrition, but has also put that knowledge into form. Have you ever seen a fat personal trainer? I never have. They are thin and muscular, and always crazy good-looking. Is this a fluke? No! They acquired the knowledge that was necessary to have a healthy body, and they act in ways to support it. They've already done the hard work. All you have to do is sweat, and do what they tell you to do. The exercises that they give you to do will give you the body that you desire. The trainers do the exercises too!

It's like I said previously in the chapter, look for the straight line to get you from where you are now, to where you want. It's like a Garmin for life. You want to get to address A from address B. The Garmin is programmed to give you the fastest and easiest path to your final destination.

Your mentor is your life Garmin!

You don't have to figure it out on your own. You just have to show up, and do what they tell you to do. It's so easy!

We are so lucky to live in the information age. There's so much knowledge on the internet that anyone can find; some of it's free, and some of it is not. Find the information that you need to achieve your goal, and follow the steps.

Don't let your ego or your past experiences stop you because they will try. Your family will want to eat pizzas on Fridays because you have always had Pizza Fridays. If you want to fit into your skinny jeans again, loading up on high-carbohydrate foods certainly won't get you there. If your family is overweight too, then it's definitely time to take charge of the situation and feed them healthier options.

There are healthy food services now that can deliver highly nutritious meals with preparation step cards right to your door, eliminating the hassle of meal prepping and shopping. There are also places called restaurants that have healthy choices that also taste great. If they didn't, they would be out of business. The chefs, like the personal trainers, have studied culinary science, and possess food prep skills and nutrition, and bring them to you. All you have to do is choose what you want, and they will prepare it for you.

Look to the experts. Look to the gurus. Look for your mentor Garmin.

It's the easiest and fastest way to reach your goal. The habits that they will teach you will totally change the course of your life. There will be daily choices that you never thought to make. Suggestions and examples of things that they've already gone through that will save you so much time, money, and effort. Piggyback off them. This is how they live, AND make their living! They know the information, and they put it to use in their own life.

You don't want to go to a person that does dentistry in their basement, right? You want to go to someone that's studied their craft and practices it every day!

Find the class, trainer, or expert, and use their knowledge as a base foundation, and build your own life skills around it.

Think of these new skills as a trampoline. As you jump, the energy you bring into your bent knees thrusts down to your feet and into the rubber trampoline base. This energy is then stopped, and returned to your body causing you to jump high into the air.

The same thing will happen with the new skills you learn from your mentor. These new skills will create awareness that you can accomplish your goal if you do certain tasks. Then all you have to do is put those skill sets in place, and you will be rewarded by accomplishing your goal.

Phil Jackson, the NBA's most highly decorated professional coach with 11 championships, mentored some of the NBA's top players of all time, such as Michael Jordan, Kobe Bryant, and Shaquille O'Neal. Even Steve Kerr, the Warrior's current coach who's won three championships so far, learned from the best. Phil studied psychology, philosophy, and religion in college. He said,

"It's not the most physically talented teams that win, it's the team that can best use its talents that wins."

He learned to take different people with different talents and personalities, and use the best of them to form an unbeatable team that would dominate anyone that came into their path.

We can do this too. Other gurus out there tell us to work on our weaknesses to try to make them better. I think this is counterproductive. What we should do is forget about the negative weaknesses, and develop our strengths.

Sometimes finding your strengths isn't so easy. I, myself didn't realize that I had a great ability to find out a complex idea, and simplify it so it could be applied, until my mentor brought this up. It was an "aha" moment, and I ran with it creating this book and the ideas in it.

Changing your habits is never an easy thing to do when you think about all the things you do wrong, and how much time and energy it will take to make a change. What the Habit Formula does is break down this complex subject into an easy-to-use process that you just make a part of your everyday routine.

If it's simple, everyone will do it!

This is how I've changed my life, my health, and my passion in life! I've figured out what I want to change, and then developed a simple plan on doing it. I didn't know every step I had to take to do it.

Why?

Because I haven't done it yet. Once I do get there, I will know how to do it, and then I'll repeat those actions to get the same results. Then I'll move on to the next. Finding a mentor can make these steps so much easier and faster!

The "how" is an easy stumbling block for most people. I am constantly racking my brain on the "how." This is where a mentor comes back into play. They've completed the journey, and have the map of steps that *you* must take to get to the next goal.

You must live in the present, and take your action steps now. If you do it today, you'll be able to create a different future.

If your mentor tells you to do "this," then do "this". If your mentor says to do "that," then do "that". Do "this" and "that" until it's done, and you've reached your goal. Doing "this" and "that" over and over again will become habitual behavior patterns that will become ingrained into your subconscious mind. This will create predictable results.

You must *do* "this" and "that". All of it. Not just a little of "this," or some of "that". You must do all of "this" and all of "that" to get to the end goal. Are you willing and able to do "this" and "that"? If so, just do what your mentor tells you to do. "This" and "that" is how they've gotten to the point that you want to be. If you start doing other things, you will change the path, and your goal will be missed.

Don't get in your own way. Leave your ego at the door. If you knew everything, you'd already be experiencing your new habit and end goal. Realize where you are right now at this moment. Learn what the next step is from your mentor, and take the next step. You will meet the goal faster and easier if you take the beaten path towards it. If you do things your way, you'll end up getting lost or ending up in the same spot as you are now, unhappy and desiring something better. Why waste any more time?

You may think the next step is trivial. Do it anyway. You may not think the next step is important. Do it anyway. The reason you are in the state that you're in now, is that you haven't realized how important each step truly is in obtaining the desired goal.

It's a not only a science, but there's also a formula to it.

Your mentor has already figured it out. While you've been stumbling and racking your brain trying to figure things out, your mentor's been enjoying the success that they deserve because they followed the correct steps needed to reach the end goal.

They've figured out how to be healthy, and have the energy to live their life. They've figured out how to be outgoing, and go after what they want instead of being shy, and watching other people live their lives. Get off your butt, find someone that knows what they're doing, and take that first step, no matter how scary it is, no matter how stupid it may seem. Do it anyways!

There's a reason and purpose for everything! Do it, and you will then be led to the next step, and the next step, until finally you're getting what you've always wanted. Then you just apply the same strategy to other areas of your life, and repeat. Find a new mentor, coach, or trainer and just follow their system. And on, and on.

Welcome to a successful life my friends. The fire is warm, come out of the cold, and join us!

The only regrets you'll have are that you didn't start earlier, you wasted a lot of time trying and failing, and you didn't believe the system would work. This is how these mentors live their lives, and make their living. They've done it, and they want to help other people do it too.

Take them up on it. Hire them. Ask them to help you. There's no shame asking for help. We're all human, and we've all needed help at some point in our lives. Be humble. Get the help you need to change those darn learned behaviors that are holding you back.

Tell them what you want, and then do what they tell you. It's so easy and simple, but not many people do it because they don't realize that they too can do it, and be successful. They allow others to influence them, and take control of their actions.

When you do this, you will always get the same results in life. Your mentor will help shatter those habits, and make you aware that there are other ways of doing things, and if you do "this" and "that," you too can reach the same success!

If you need a mentor to show you how to change your habits following *The Habit Formula*, go to my website at www.thehabitformula.com and see which program is right for you.

Assignment #4

A. Look back at your list of goals from Chapter 3. List 5 people or programs that can help you achieve your goals faster. Build your mentor list.

Example List:

1. Organize garage – My mother, who is awesome at organization.

2. Vacation – someone from the family that loves to plan trips or travel guide.

3. Lose 20 pounds – join gym, start swimming, join a class, get involved with a league.

4. Pay off credit cards – get with employer or bank and set up automatic payments to pay your debt so you won't even know it's missing.

5. Get promotion – look for someone who is already doing your new job and ask them for guidance. Your boss, he/she can tell you what you have to do.

Chapter 5
Choices

$$A + D + M + \boxed{C} + P = HM$$

Step #4 to Habit Mastery = Choices
This is the action chapter!

This is the actual part of the book where your life begins to change!

You should be very excited! I don't care whether you've read the rest of the book or you skipped right to this chapter. Either way, it's now time for action.

Pick something to change. If you do this, you will get a different result, and your life will start to change. If you don't, you will be in the same place tomorrow, next week, and even next year as you are today.

Nothing is difficult or impossible!

You need to focus a little time and a little energy towards changing a habit, and that time and energy will multiply your results.

Let's say you want to change two habits: being late and being overweight. They seem like they have nothing to do with one another, but they work in synergy. If you're always late, you probably feel sluggish by the end of the day because you've used anxiety cortisol levels to rush around, and try to make it on time. After a few minutes of adrenaline, your body goes into recovery mode, and you come off your runner's high.

This is the same feeling as being overweight. A little exertion totally depletes your body of energy, and your mind takes over and you don't feel like doing anything. You then plop on the couch, and watch TV all night.

Also being late and being overweight have a lack of "future planning" as a common theme. You may think that something is going to take a certain amount of time to accomplish, but it runs over, and that snowballs other appointments until you run out of time for the day.

Being overweight can be like that too. You skip a meal because you're working on a project. Soon, you feel famished, and you go through the fast food drive-thru just to get something in your belly.

It's a lack of planning. If you change one habit that's not serving you, you can pick up traits, thoughts, and other behavior patterns that can affect other habits that you want to change.

I learned that by eating differently. I've began to think about my life differently, and those thoughts have started to snowball the change in my results in other areas of my life, just by changing one habit.

You will find the same thing happens for you. That's why you should start with something small – something you know you can change, and won't take a lot of time, energy, or thought to change it. If you build up your confidence, you can easily start going after the bigger habits that will totally change your life!

The saying goes, "If you fail to plan, you plan to fail."

I'm not saying that you're failing in life. No matter where you're starting from, you can change it. You just have to work on it every day. Even on the weekends. Even on the holidays. Just do it every day.

I work on my business goals during the three days that I'm at the office. I work on my seminars, books, and programs two days a week, and I work on my personal goals every day! I've noticed the past couple of years, that I have changed my life so much, that I wouldn't recognize myself a couple of years ago. It just keeps getting better! It will do the same for you.

Start right now, today! Get a notebook and write out these questions. Do it over the weekend, after the kids are in bed, or you have a spare hour to answer them. Be honest with yourself, and see your life where you are now. The only thing you can change is now.

Answer these questions.

Steps to change your habits:

1. Are you happy where you are?
2. Are you happy with what you've become?
3. Are you happy with how much money you make?

4. Are you happy with how you look?

5. Are you happy with how you feel?

6. If not, why?

7. What's holding you back?

8. Who and what is talking you out of pursuing your image of yourself and your life?

We've got a short time on this planet. Some have a shorter time than others. There's no signed contract that says everyone has 100+ years on this planet, and then you're done.

There's also no signed contract that says each one of us should be married, or have a loving partner, make tons of money, and have a hot, attractive, healthy body. If you're happy, awesome! I'm not sure why you're reading this book, if you're 100% happy with your life. My hunch, is that you're not happy or satisfied with something in your life. The question is, why?

What are you going to do about it? Why are you letting your bad habits control your life? Who cares about your failing past experiences that never seemed to work out? You will start doing things differently, and will learn from someone who is successful. They will teach you how to be more successful too.

Don't give up! Not giving up will become your first new habit. Don't quit! Keep learning new things, and begin to change your behavior patterns, and ultimately your life! It's very simple to do. Just pick something to change, and start changing it. It's all about daily practice. Just don't quit! Make things simple and easy! Do the easy stuff on your list.

Professional basketball players constantly practice the easy stuff. They call these skills fundamentals. Dribbling. Passing the ball. Free throws. There's no difference between the fundamentals at a professional level, and those at a high school level. The difference is how well those fundamental skills are executed.

The professionals still have to dribble. They still have to pass. They still have to make jump shots, box out, jump, and rebound. These people have practiced these fundamental skills so much during their lives that they have developed muscle memory. Their body knows what to do if they want to dunk the ball. They've done those movements thousands of times. Now they don't even think about it, they involuntarily just do it.

This is the same thing we're going to do with our minds. We're going to brainwash ourselves, and develop mind muscle memory so that we will practice our behavioral patterns over and over again until they become involuntary habits. These habits will lead us to our goals.

We're going to "wash" away your past experiences, your opinions about the world and how it works, and your environmental upbringing that helped mold your behavior that has set the course for your life.

You will soon learn that YOU are your biggest obstacle.

The biggest lesson to learn at the start is to get out of your own way. You may come from a bad neighborhood. You may be rich. You may be fat. You may be depressed. You may come from a family that doesn't support you. You may be in an abusive relationship. You know what? It doesn't matter! You don't need any money or a certain pedigree to improve yourself.

You just need to give yourself permission to do it, and then decide that you will change the habits that are preventing you from living the life you want to live. This is what this book is all about. Getting you to shut off your mind of your surroundings, your past, your family, and your friends that have held you back from being the person who you want to be.

I am raising my child to be free, and pursue whatever he wants in life. If he wants to be a dentist like me, it would be great, and I've given him a path to follow. If he wants to do something else, I will encourage him to find a mentor, and follow that path that will lead him to his goals.

Stop getting in your own way!

We're going to start right here, right now today! If you want me to lead you step by step into this with a workbook and videos, go to my website www.thehabitformula.com and either sign up for the program or group coaching sessions.

If you think you've got this, then grab a new fresh page in your notebook and let's get started.

I want you to answer the following questions:

<u>Choose one small habit that you want to change.</u>

Start with something small, so that you can achieve it easily and quickly creating confidence and momentum. You will do this personally and professionally. Just pick one thing personally and professionally that you want to change, and let's start taking actions to change it!

1. **What habit do you WANT to change?**

   A. Professionally-

   B. Personally-

2. **What habit do you NEED to change to get the results you want?**

   A. Professionally-

   B. Personally-

Sometimes what you *want* to change, may not necessarily be what you *need* to change to get the results that you want. Sometimes you need to look at things in a different perspective.

I WANT more money, but I NEED to build my follow-up skills to reconnect with previous clients that either bought from me previously, or just said no. If you change the bad habit of not following up, your sales will increase, thus paying you more commissions!

You have to dig deeper to what really will make the difference in your results. That's what the second question is all about, digging a little bit deeper, and really looking at a habit that will change your results.

3. **What benefits will you receive if you change this habit?**

   A. Professionally-

   B. Personally-

4. **Why haven't you changed this habit?**

   A. Professionally-

B. Personally-

5. How can you change it?

A. Professionally-

B. Personally-

6. Who can influence you positively in creating this new habit?

A. Professionally-

B. Personally-

7. How long will it take for your new habit to form?

A. Professionally-

B. Personally-

8. When do you want to get started forming your new habit?

A. Professionally-

B. Personally-

Here's an example of a list I came up with:

1. What habit do you WANT to change?

A. Professionally- Having a morning meeting before patients arrive

B. Personally- Organize closet

2. What habit do you NEED to change to get the results you want?

A. Professionally- Arriving early to get the office organized before patients arrive

B. Personally- Get rid of stuff in closet that I don't use

3. What benefits will you receive if you change this habit?

A. Professionally- Know what the plan is for the day. Talk about irregularities to help better prepare for them. Keep everyone on the same track.

B. Personally- Less cluttered and easier to find and match outfits.

4. Why haven't you changed this habit?

A. Professionally- Lazy, never saw the value in doing it. Never knew how to run a morning meeting- what to include in it.

B. Personally- lazy. Never saw the value in having organized outfits or shelves.

5. How can you change it?

A. Professionally- Make spreadsheet covering topics that should be done in meeting and come in earlier.

B. Personally- Grab trash bags and boxes- donate what I don't want or can't fit into

6. Who can influence you positively in creating this new habit?

A. Professionally-staff needs to come in earlier too, and see the value in what we're doing, and contribute to it every morning

B. Personally- can have my mother come over to help- she's awesome at organizing things

7. How long will it take for your new habit to form?

A. Professionally- 1 week- to create spreadsheet and then schedule the team early

B. Personally- a weekend. Then once it's done, it's easier to keep up with.

8. When do you want to get started forming your new habit?

A. Professionally- Start creating spreadsheet today. Start morning meetings 1 week from today.

B. Personally- This weekend or when my mother can come over to help.

Ok. Now you know all the reasons that you *should* change your habit. You know *what* it is that you want to accomplish. You know *why* you should change it and all the benefits that come with changing it. You know *why* you *haven't* changed it already. You know *how* you can change it. You know if someone can help your process of change. You know *how long* you think it will take to accomplish your goal. And finally, you've decided *when* you're going to take action to work towards your goal.

Now it's time to take action!

This is where you start to fade, and your eyes get glossy and hazy, and your old habits and laziness return, and you never get started. You don't know how. It's very easy!

Our next and final task is to create a to-do list. That's it! A simple to-do list. It will be very short, and will not contain anything difficult to accomplish on this list. Ever! This list must be short and simple, or you will never cross things off! Even *I* won't get into something new if it's going to be hard and tedious. Let's get started!

Write down 3 things – actions, thoughts, choices – that you can do today that will get you closer to achieving your goal/end result.

Get your notebook out again and write this down:

My habit: _____

Today I will:

1.

2.

3.

Here's my example of my to-do list:

My habit: Morning Huddle

Today I will:

1. Make a list of questions I want to include during the meeting

2. Figure out how long the meeting will be

3. Figure out when the meeting will start.

That's it! This is just today's list. Tomorrow's list will be completely different. This will be an ongoing thing. You know what your end goal or habit is, and now you're starting to learn *how* to create it.

Sometimes you have a mentor to give you the list, and sometimes you have to figure it out on your own. Either way, just do three things that don't take much time or effort, and you will notice that you will consistently get closer and closer to your end result.

Let's look at my list for my personal goal:

My habit: Become organized – start with closet

Today I will:

1. Buy some hangers to get wanted clothes hung up on racks

2. Get some trash bags and boxes

3. Schedule a pick-up for the donations

How hard was that? It literally took me ten seconds to figure out three things I could do today to help me get ready to organize my closet. It didn't take a lot of time, and I know I can cross off all three things on my list successfully!

I'm not too busy to go to Walmart, and buy some hangers and trash bags, or go behind my local warehouse club, and grab some free boxes. These first three things are critical, and lay the foundation for my organization day to go fast and smoothly.

If I have extra hangers, I can hang things up that are crunched up on the floor. If I have bags and boxes ready to go, I can easily start going through shoes, accessories, and clothes, and just put them in the appropriate bags and boxes for either donations or trash.

So easy! You can do this too! Start out with something simple and fast. Like cleaning out your car, or paying your bills. Maybe you want to start with doing laundry, or cleaning off your desk at work.

Accomplish something easy! When you do this, you will become confident that you can do anything you set your mind to. Then you can move onto bigger and harder habits, like saving money, losing weight, or going back to school so you can move onto a higher paying job.

Even though there are bigger and harder habits that you would like to change, just simplify your everyday tasks and daily choices. They will lead to bigger and better things!

You must take a step back, and ask yourself why you want to organize your closet? What does this really mean? Well, most people who are well-organized with their material possessions, are also well-organized in their general life. Their thought patterns move them towards organizing their ideas and behavior patterns, so that everything comes out orderly. When things are orderly, stress levels are minimalized. You're not always rushing around trying to find things. You know where things are, and you're more prepared. Being prepared is a great habit to have, and being organized is, too.

By simply cleaning out your closet, you're setting yourself up for success! You can get ready for work faster in the morning because you can find the outfit that you want. You know that everything fits and looks good, and you can move onto bigger things.

When you're prepared, others will look to you for answers. They know that you've organized the ideas and issues that have been brought up, and they will seek you out. This will, in turn, make you invaluable at your job, which usually turns into a higher paying position and more money.

I am very organized in my office. All the drawers are clearly marked, and all the instruments are grouped together for a certain procedure. I use the same instruments, and do the procedures the same way every day. This makes the process go very smoothly. My patients always comment at how fast and good we did things. Organization and being prepared definitely helps with this. We know what we're doing, and we simplify things.

If it's not a habit, make it one. You can make a lot more money, and have a lot more time if you have it!

Start slowly. Start with a closet, a dresser, or a desk. Once you see the value in it, you will move onto other areas that need to be tidied up. You'll soon see that you're in the habit of keeping things organized, and you won't even consciously think about it anymore. A few small tasks done every day can lead to big things that can change your life forever!

Sometimes, you have only one list of three daily tasks that you must repeat over and over again until you get the results that you're looking for.

Another example of a habit: living debt-free

Today I will:

1. Bring a packed lunch to work and put the $10 towards paying off debt.

2. Carpool or take public transportation

3. If it's Friday, make extra weekly payment on credit card.

These three tasks may need to be repeated daily every day, until the debt is paid off.

Your list is easy to follow and you won't even have to think about it after a couple of weeks. You'll form the habit of just doing it, and you'll see your debt disappear before your eyes.

I did this myself when I had student loans and business debt to pay off. It worked, and I didn't feel like I was sacrificing too much. I just made different choices every day, until finally I was debt free!

If you need more help with these lists, or need me to hold your hand, go to www.thehabitformula.com and check out my other programs and coaching. No matter where you start, you will take one step closer to getting the results you want. You must decide *that you want* to change, decide *what you want* to change, and decide *which three steps you want to take today,* to bring you closer to that goal.

Three things today will lead to 1095 steps by this time next year! You will find that most things don't take you 1095 steps to take. Sometimes it will only take three steps repeated over and over again for a few weeks, and then that habit is changed for good! You may find that you take 300 steps for this problem to be solved. If your next habit is related to the first one, it may only take you 100 steps more to reach that one, because you were nearly at the end.

Most people start thinking about goals near the holidays because of the New Year, but usually fail in doing anything about them in the first couple of weeks in January. Then they still don't revisit these goals until the end of the year. They start the New Year in the exact same spot that they started the old one, without change.

If you start working on a new habit today, you will be amazed at how many things you accomplish in a year from now! 1095 steps towards multiple goals is awesome! You will have everything written out, and all you have to do is read your list, do the tasks on it, and cross them off.

It's *so simple* and *powerful,* yet most people never accomplish anything.

When you put these thoughts on paper, it's out of your mind, and it is present in the universe. Then you can have it in front of you, and read it every day. You can proceed with action. It's already out there so you all you have to do is take action.

Don't let your social influences, your past, your environment, or your family change your mind, or discourage you. It's already out of your mind, and now you can focus on making it come true.

If it's written down on physical paper, it now is part of the physical world. You can see the words with your own eyes. You can feel the paper. It's not inside of you where your self-doubt and old bad habits can cause it to die.

Being part of the physical world gives your tasks and ideas life.

Then all you have to do is live the life. You've already written your path, now just live it! That's why I want you to write them all down on paper. Pick the easy ones you want to tackle first, the ones that have fewer steps, and can be accomplished faster.

With the new habits you form from the easy ones, you'll see that they lead into different daily choices that will lead you to succeed at the bigger ones.

It's like compounding interest. One choice made now, can affect multiple habits until one day, the ones you thought you would never change, will be gone, and your life will then never be the same.

I never thought I would enjoy writing as much as I do. I have a knack for simplifying things, and creating efficient systems that make my life easier. I've been making to-do lists since I was a young person. I would see the end results, and then make lists of actions that I would need to take to get the end result. I would always work backwards from my goals.

Sometimes all the steps weren't necessary. Sometimes the steps I thought were needed were the wrong steps, and I either had to change them, or I had to abandon my thoughts on achieving those results. It seems like every time I want to change something, I make a physical list, and I start moving in the direction that I want.

To simplify this book, I only wanted to include three steps at a time. I realize that if the list gets too long, you will just do the simple stuff, and you will never get to the hard stuff. I do this too. In other words, make it simple! If you do, you will surely succeed!

Furthering your education, training for a new job, opening a new business, losing weight, and living a healthy lifestyle, will take some time to accomplish, but keep your daily choices simple, and directed towards your end result.

You can make this list before bed or in the morning before your day gets started. As long as you have a plan, you can then focus your energy on it, and accomplish it. Sometimes, your list will be things you can check off right away in the morning. Sometimes, you may have to get to work to start working on them. Like making extra sales calls, organizing your files, or creating your next meeting presentation.

As long as you accomplish it by the end of the day, congratulations, you did it! Tomorrow, make another list, or follow the same one as today, but do it!

You will find that you will start feeling differently.

Your previous anxiety will slowly melt away because your bad habits are starting to change into good ones. You never want to be fighting the current. You do this when you have a bad habit. There's a lot of anxiety, flight or fight, and negativity that surrounds bad habits. When you're making different daily choices that change these behavior patterns, you will find that the universe just seems easier. People are friendlier, and your stress level decreases.

That's because you're learning to follow the current of the universe, and the universe is acknowledging your changes, and rewarding you because of them. That's how the universe works. If you put positivity out there, you'll get positivity back. You'll start losing weight, and your energy levels will increase. Your friends and family will compliment you and ask you how you're doing it.

Your boss will notice your new sales skills and put you in charge of a team of sales people, or even give you a new position. You'll earn more money. You'll also save more money because you have no more debt. You'll feel more secure in life because you'll be debt-free, and have a compounding nest egg that will be there when you're old and gray. You'll feel more confident that you can accomplish anything you set your mind to, and the universe will begin to notice.

Your contact list will grow exponentially. People will want to do business with you. You will gain the confidence necessary to know that the skills you've developed can help so many people. Now that sounds like a great life to me!

No one says you have to be perfect! I certainly am not! I make a list every day, and work on things I want to improve about myself. Isn't that what life is? A journey? Sometimes, it's a little rough and bumpy. Sometimes, you go down the wrong path, but you can easily straighten out your course of action.

Nothing will change until you make up your mind that you want to change something.

Then make a list of what you want to change. Make a list of your daily actions, and the changes will result. Having the power to change takes a lot of courage and perseverance. It will be easy at first. As you move onto harder goals, you will face more difficult challenges and obstacles.

Don't worry – just keep working on your tasks every day. You will succeed if you continue working on it. If you have a mentor, just follow the steps they laid out for you. Keep working on it. They already figured it out, you don't need to reinvent the wheel. Simply do what they tell you.

If you need to change your diet, either find a restaurant that has the foods that are on your diet and eat there constantly, or find a cookbook that follows your diet and make those recipes. These people have already figured it out! Eat this way, and your body will change! Follow the recipes or eating plan every day. If you have a favorite meal that's not on your plan, recreate it following the foods you are allowed to eat.

This is what I've done with my keto diet: I eat cookies and donuts every day, and I've lost 20 pounds! They are special keto cookies and donut recipes, high fat and low carb. I still eat cookies and donuts; they are just made differently than the traditional ones. Do you understand? I follow the different recipes, and I get different results!

It really wasn't difficult, especially with the internet. I learned the basic rules for the diet, the foods I could eat, and started buying those foods at the market. It's just a different way of cooking.

So, this whole book is about getting you to think differently. Not allowing your past experience, your customs, your environment, or the people around you to influence your behaviors.

It's in these places that you learned these habits to begin with, and are also responsible for the results you're getting.

Now it's time to think differently. You may think you're going against the current because your outside influences will try to stop you from changing, but you'll soon notice that things will become so much easier the more steps you take towards your goals. It's almost like the universe will start opening up to you.

You will find out how your perception will change. You'll become more open-minded towards new ideas and thoughts. Some of which will help you succeed in your goals.

You'll find that your environment will soon change because you won't have anything in common with your old friends, and you'll find a new inner circle that you can grow with. It's okay to let go of the past. It's okay to start looking into the future, and planning your present so you can get there.

You will find that you'll build newer and stronger habitual behaviors that will improve your life in ways you may not have thought. All of this can be yours, if you start today with a simple list of three choices or tasks you want to take towards your goal.

Three simple actions will lay down the giant foundation that will hold your new habitual behavior. If you make these three choices every day, you will start to see that anything is possible. No matter how many times you've tried in the past, no matter how fat you feel, no matter if you think that goal is for someone else, it's now time to prove everyone and everything that's holding you back, is wrong!

If this simple girl from a tiny town in Ohio can dream big dreams, and help people from all around the world with simple concepts like what I've shared with you today, then anything is possible! Anyone can do it! Anyone can improve themselves. It starts and ends with you! I can't do it for you. I can help *guide* you, but *you* must be the one to act.

Act now! Make your lists now! Start today!

If you start today, by the end of the week, month, and year, think of where you'll be? You'll end up shocking yourself at where you'll end up. All the people who have held you back will want to change too, because they'll see that you're getting positive results, and they'll want that for themselves!

Remember that this is an abundant world!

There's enough skinny clothes, money, education, clients, and general happiness for everyone! You need to decide what you want out of your life, then take action every day towards that goal! If you make it simple, you will have no excuse to not do it! Start right now!

If you need help, go to www.thehabitformula.com, and I can guide you every step of the way!

Start today, and your life will be different too!

Assignment #5

Choose your first goal/habit and then pick 3 daily activities/tasks/choices that you can do to help you reach your goal. Every day you will choose 3 tasks/activities/choices until you reach your habit/goal. Do this both professionally and personally.

Example List:

Professional Habit: Become more organized – start w/ garage

3 choices/tasks/activities:

1. Buy cabinets, hooks, bins

2. Arrange time for mom to come over and help.

3. Make a simple drawing of my cabinet layout.

Personal Habit: Lose weight

3 choices/tasks/activities

1. Make keto cookies

2. Go to tae kwon do

3. Don't eat any bread today

Chapter 6
Persistence

$$A + D + M + C + \boxed{P} = HM$$

Step #5 to Habit Mastery = Persistence

You need to keep your three daily tasks in your mind as much as possible. If you don't focus or concentrate on the one habit you want to change, the energy you're putting into that habit will dissipate, and your mind will soon forget about it.

Have you ever had a great idea?

If only I could ____.

I want to do ____.

I wish I had ____.

We've all done this.

The question becomes how many times did you get ____, or did ____, or became ____? Most of the time, you wanted it, but you didn't keep your focus on obtaining it.

You let other things get in your way. "I'll go there when I have the money." "I'll stop doing this after the holidays." "I'll do that when I lose 10 pounds." It seems like we constantly give ourselves ultimatums for an activity. This is where that darn Law of Cause and Effect comes into play again.

We know from Chapter 3 that the Law of Cause and Effect states that every effect has a definite cause. Your thoughts, behaviors, and actions create specific effects that create your life as you perceive it. Your senses, then, are engaged at things around you, and that's the life that you're aware of. It's almost like having blinders on. You know that there are other things going on around you, but only *you* can experience what you can see right in front of you.

Our minds can only handle so much stimuli at a time. Have you ever used perfume or cologne and put too much on? After a few minutes, you can't even smell it, but when you walk into a room filled with people, the people around you notice that it's very strong, and make you aware of it again.

That's perception. Your nose picks up the smell, and sends the signal to your brain, but after a while, the signal to your brain becomes weaker because there's something else that comes into your sensory field, and your brain moves onto that object.

The same thing can happen when we're doing our daily actions towards our habitual behaviors. "Oh, I'll just have a little cake today, I've been so good." Tomorrow it is, "I won't go to the gym today because I've had a hard day and I'm tired, I'll go tomorrow."

Instead of focusing your behavior towards your goal of losing weight, now you're allowing your mind to wander to something else, and you're losing focus on your main objective, which is to lose weight.

Have you ever been in a room with another person without hearing a word that they said to you? It's not that there weren't sound waves that were being created by the other person's vocal cords and mouth. It's that you didn't allow your brain to pick up on those sound waves. You could physically *hear* them, but you weren't mentally *listening* to them.

There's a big difference here, and it all comes down to your perception. Your awareness of your environment, and how you let that environment influence your senses, your thoughts, and your actions. You must also be aware of your choices, tasks, and activities because they are responsible for your behavior patterns that lead to your results. It's the realization of your thoughts and actions that drives your end goals.

The whole process of changing your bad habits isn't the difficult part. The part of it that's difficult is sticking with it. Focusing and dedicating your attention to doing it every day. That's the difficulty of the whole process.

Daily persistence.

This is why you must write down three daily tasks on your to-do list and the main goal every day.

Even if it's the same three daily tasks that you're repeating until you reach your end goal. When you physically write them down, you're not only stimulating your brain by seeing the tasks, and feeling the pen while you're writing and holding the paper, but you're also using your body to physically write it down. You're putting your mind and body in motion on a concentrated thing, and you're joining the two forces together to get an end result: your written tasks. Just this activity alone will get you in a state of focus.

You are bringing your awareness and attention to those three daily tasks that you must accomplish today if you are to change what it is that you are unhappy with in your life. They are real. They are physically written on a piece of paper. You can actually touch the paper. They're not just locked up in the corner of your mind in a place that you can easily forget, while you go about your daily routine. They're out there, in the world, for you to focus on.

You will then read these three daily tasks, and physically cross them off, one by one, as you fulfill them. This will also combine your physical and mental powers towards your goals.

Your goal today must be to cross those three daily tasks off your list, and this will help keep you focused.

Don't look into the future, and think about how long this goal is going to take to reach. That's not the purpose of making your list. The purpose of making your list is to give you something that will move you in the direction you want to take. You must take action every day. That's all. Nothing more, nothing less.

Your mentor, if you have one, told you to do these three things. Go ahead and do them. You need to start moving, and the only way to do that is to take one step at a time. That's what today is about. The first step is to cross off your three daily tasks. Don't worry about tomorrow yet, because you're not aware how the three daily accomplishments will affect what your next steps will be tomorrow, and beyond.

"The game has its ups and downs, but you can never lose focus of your individual goals, and you can't let yourself be beat because of lack of effort." – Michael Jordan

It's the A-for-effort kind of thing. You will always succeed if you put the effort in. You may not succeed right away. You may have a hundred different obstacles in your way, but you must put in the effort to get around them so that you can do what you really want to do in life. Living the way you want is a matter of your own thinking and doing.

Don't allow outside distractions to get in your way! No one has the right to kill your dreams! You can accomplish your dreams without hurting anyone else. There's an infinite supply of everything, you just have to know your end goal and work at it every day until you reach it.

Sometimes, you will find that today's daily tasks will open up different possibilities and paths for you to discover. Maybe, your main goal is to learn more effective communication skills when selling your products to your clients. You may find that, during this process, a new position opens up that requires you to make company presentations to other groups interested in working with your company. You're already working on your communication skills in a smaller environment. Now you may expand those skills to include a bigger audience with visual and video props. Your blinders have expanded a little, and you can broaden your focus and build on the skills that you already were working on.

You never know what opportunity is around the corner. If you didn't focus your attention on advancing your communication skills, you would have missed out on a potential new job with more money and new responsibilities that could lead you to even bigger things in the future. This goes back to the Law of Cause and Effect: one thing causes something else to happen.

Instead of playing victim to it, you can start controlling it and using it for your own purposes.

You are the one that's in total control of your life!

Dedicate yourself to changing the things that you don't like in your life. Focus attention each and every day on accomplishing your three daily tasks. Every day. Even holidays. Even your birthday. Even the weekends. Just do it.

You'll be so amazed at how much you *can* accomplish if you put the wheels of momentum in your favor.

Remember the Law of Momentum or Newton's 1st Law from Physics class? I always hated that class, but now I embrace these laws, and use them to my advantage!

Newton's 1st Law states that any object will move in the direction where constant force is applied, if the constant force pushing it is greater than the opposite dragging force. In other words, an object will remain at rest, until something makes it move, and an object will remain in motion until something stops it.

We can use this to our advantage towards breaking our debilitating habits. Right now, you're living your life as you are, but you're struggling to achieve what you want. You're overweight. You're struggling to make more money. You're still single and long for a loving long-term relationship. Basically, you're at rest.

The only way for you to start moving in the direction that you want, is literally to start moving in that direction.

This is what the previous chapter was all about: the action steps! Getting your physical and mental energy moving towards your goal. Writing down, accomplishing, and crossing off your three daily tasks.

This "momentum" will continue, until you stop doing those three daily tasks. When you stop doing your three daily tasks, you will no longer be moving towards your goal and, in fact, could start moving backwards towards your starting point. No one wants to do that! The only thing that will stop your momentum is YOU!

If you're overweight and only one dress makes you look and feel confident, and your sister takes it, you might want to skip that networking event and blame her for it. Don't. Go buy another dress!

Don't blame the job market for your lack of finding work — you can work on developing skills that are in demand in your area that will land you a new job.

Don't let anyone or anything stop your momentum!

Keep your focus on your daily tasks, and keep the blinders on. This will eliminate distractions that will always try to sabotage your progress. This doesn't mean that you can't have fun in life, or you can't enjoy doing some shopping, or eating a piece of cake once in a while, or stay in your jammies all day and veg out.

You have to stay *on* target *more* than you stay *off* target.

Hang out, relax, and watch TV *only* after your three daily tasks are done. You can go to the party, and go dancing with your friends *only* after you check off your three daily tasks. You can rest and relax, but you still have to take another step. If you do this, it will build a daily habit of doing your daily list. See how one habit can form another?

They are all connected, and together, they create your personality and your attitude. Your thoughts, feelings, and actions make up your attitude. While changing one habit, you will certainly change others, and before you know it, you'll be a better 2.0 version of yourself, and you will look back on the past year, and you won't even recognize yourself. You will have accomplished so many things that in prior years you couldn't even conceive.

That's what this whole book has been about. Getting you to focus on what you want, and exactly how to do it. Most people think that the "how" is usually the *hard* part, and is the part that stops you before you even get started.

Now you know that the "how" is actually the *easy* part of changing your habits. The "how" is just taking one step at a time towards your end result. Each step consists of three daily tasks that you will focus your attention and energy on until you achieve them.

The hard part about changing your habits is actually dedication, keeping yourself focused on the "how", and putting in the effort every day. It's called persistence. Don't let outside influences, your environment, your family and friends, your customs, or your past experiences block your desire to change.

The reasons you have these habits that you want to change are the same reasons that will keep you from changing them.

This is all common sense, but sometimes common sense is not so common! Don't let that happen! Have laser focus every day on those three daily tasks.

Yes, you have to run the kids to soccer practice. Yes, you have to travel out of town for a meeting. Yes, you must clean out the garage for the party this weekend. You're always going to have things that you need to do to keep your life moving. If you want to accomplish a new goal or change a bad habit that's not giving you the results you want, you must carve out some time and energy every day, and focus your attention on these daily tasks.

You're worth it!

If you're in a bad relationship, a bad environment, or a bad place mentally, it's time for a change. Go back to Chapter 5, start answering the eight questions on what habits you want to change, and figure out what goals you want to accomplish. Then write down three daily tasks that you're going to accomplish today. Focus some time, energy, and attention *today* on completing those three tasks.

We all have the same amount of time in a day, a week, a month, and a year. However, not all of us have the same time in life. If this doesn't scare you a little, it should. It should help to create urgency in your mission: an urgency that you must get off your butt, go to the store, grab the nicotine product from the shelf, and start using it to help with the cravings that you'll have as you wean yourself from tobacco. You know that stuff is bad.

You know it will kill you in a horrible way. Don't wait another minute, get moving!

Your lack of time could also create an urgency to lose those extra pounds so you can get off your diabetic and high blood pressure medications, and enjoy your kids and grandkids. You need to play with them and create lasting memories that not only *you* will have, but *they* will have the rest of their lives!

If you don't dedicate your time and energy towards making more money so that you can support your kids, and give them a positive fulfilling life, who will? When will you do it? When they're 50?

Now's the time to use momentum in your favor. All you have to do is take the next step. It's not that difficult. It won't cost you a lot of time or money. The rewards are endless as long as you keep taking the next step!

Just one at a time.

To quote Dory from the Disney movie *Finding Nemo*, "Just keep swimming, just keep swimming."

You may not know exactly *why* you're taking the next step. The answers will present themselves at a later time, and you will be so thankful and grateful that you took the next step. It's called momentum. Your lack of time causes urgency to start moving in the direction of your goal. Momentum will then cause a belief that you can change the habits or behavior patterns that have gotten you in your present state.

Persistence will help you dedicate some energy, love, money, and time to getting what you want. It will also help you change the things that are holding you back in your life. These are all essential to reaching your goals.

If you do the tasks that are different, and move in directions that you've never moved before, you will start living in a different way. You will see that these movements will become habits, leading you to the discovery of new and better things that are out in the world. Things you've never seen or experienced before.

Persistence. Every day!

Assignment #6

This is another exercise along with those from Chapter 5 that you must do every day. If you don't, your desires to change will slowly fade, and next year you'll be right where you are now.

- A. At the end of the day, did you accomplish your 3 daily activities/tasks/choices?

    1. Yes – awesome – keep up the good work! You will achieve your goal very soon!

    2. No – why not? Can you accomplish them tomorrow? If yes, then finish your list tomorrow and keep it going. If no, you must ask yourself if you really want to change, or are you letting something distract you or hold you back? Get rid of those things and get back on track! No one is responsible for your changes except you!

- B. How long have you been working on your goal?
- C. Are you close to getting it done?

The activities in this chapter are about cheerleading and accountability. Without it, you're dead in the water. Following through is *the* most difficult thing to do, but it is necessary for you to succeed. Winners never quit!

Chapter 7
Habit Mastery

$A + D + M + C + P = \boxed{HM}$

Final Step #6 is to become a Habit Master

So now you've done it! You've achieved at least the first five of your goals that you wrote down in Chapter 1. You've done what was asked of you, and you didn't stop until you succeeded!

Congratulations! You did it! I knew you could!

I'm sure there were a lot of doubters around you, including yourself at times, but you closed them off, and now you're moving in the right direction.

Now what?

Repeat the formula over and over again in every area of your life!

Isn't this what life is about? Living each day to its fullest? How can you do this when you allow other people, things, and beliefs to stop you from doing the things that you truly want to do? Or the dreams that you have? Why hide? Let these things out.

I have discovered my love of writing. I've written a few articles that have been published in national and international dental journals. I've had people ask me, "How did you do it?" I just literally contacted the editor, and asked how to do it, and then did what they said. It was so easy and so gratifying to see my name and picture printed for all my peers to see. By doing this process in my own life, I've discovered that there really is a habit formula that I can use in every aspect of my life.

I choose a goal or habit that I want to obtain. I find a mentor, which I've discovered is the *easiest* and *fastest* way to accomplish anything, and I make my list of three daily tasks that align me with my goal and do them. You can too! I've done all the legwork! Follow the formula, do the assignments at the end of each chapter, and get your mind and your body in motion!

Remember that momentum is a wonderful thing when you use it to your advantage.

When you first start moving, you may not accumulate many rewards. You haven't lost any weight after two weeks of doing your new workout routine. What you don't realize, is that you are not losing weight because you are gaining muscle. Muscle weighs more than fat, and eventually that new muscle will start using the energy from that stored fat to help you lose weight. Then you will have a more permanent weight loss.

I'm starting my new sales job, but I'm not closing a lot of clients, so I'm not making a lot of money yet. *Yet* is the operative word. You're still learning! You're still growing your sales skills.

Growth equals experience.

Once you have some experience under your belt, your sales skills will improve. All of a sudden, so will your commissions! It will happen like a water dam that's being filled too fast until it eventually bursts. It has to. You're doing the work. You're following the path. The only result that can happen is to reach your goal, to change your habit, to gain mastery. There's no other way the universe works.

Take the steps necessary to find your path. Then enjoy the rewards of your labor. When you repeat these steps over and over again, you will begin to see the patterns that slowly develop, and you will become more experienced in receiving the rewards. Then you can expand your knowledge and skill sets from there.

It's an ongoing journey. You may think that your end result or goal is really the end of your journey, but it's not. It's just the beginning. Your mind will start to think of other areas in your life that you are lacking, and the desire in you will want more. That's how humans are made.

We *always* want more. There's nothing wrong with this. Why shouldn't we have anything that we want? Why shouldn't we live the life that we dream? If we do the work, and put in the time and effort for our troubles, why shouldn't we be rewarded? We're not hurting anyone else. In most cases, we are helping other people with our services, products, and skills. In most cases we are getting out of our own way and learning how to fly in life.

Don't you feel an obligation to help other people? Don't you feel an obligation to push yourself to your new goals so that your family will benefit as well as your surrounding community and your clients? You should. You should make it your mission in life to, "Be all that you can be," a quote from the US Army.

Why would you live a lesser life? A life that has no meaning? You are born, you scrounge around for 70 years, and then you die. What's your tombstone going to say about you? What's your obituary going to say about you? Have you ever thought of your legacy on earth? I have.

I want to be known as a kind and loving person. A funny person. An upbeat person. The life of the party that everyone wants to be friends with. An honest person. Someone tough-as-nails who is dependable and can get the job done. Someone that followed her dreams, and didn't allow anyone or anything from holding her back. Someone that was wealthy, not only in the material world, but also the spiritual world. Someone who gave all of herself to as many people as she could meet.

It's nothing complex. I think there are a lot of people that want the same things. I want to leave a legacy for my son, and be someone he can look up to. I want to show my son that he can do anything in life, he just has to learn how. He needs to follow a mentor that can show him the way to a wonderful life.

Who doesn't want that? **In order to do this, you have to become a master at changing the habits that are holding you back, and learn the new ones that will sling you forward to tremendous wealth, health, and happiness.**

Are you ready? If you've read this entire book, I *know* you are ready. You just didn't know how. If you've read this entire book, *now* you know how to do it!

Invest the time, the money, and the energy into changing yourself. Your spouse may not understand why. Your family may not understand why. Your best friend may not understand why. Who cares? As long as *you* understand why, that's all that matters.

You're not asking *them* to change. You're asking *you* to change! Once you learn the process, you can then understand that you are willing and able to change. You can accomplish anything, and start to achieve mastery. Once you do that, you're off to the races.

Throughout this entire journey of writing this book, I myself have become a master of changing my limitations. These limitations were never real. They never existed except in my own head. No one in my family ever went to graduate school until I did. Now, I have numerous family members with multiple degrees, who are doing what they love to do.

No one did it until I did it. I just followed the path in front of me. I took the classes that they told me to take, and voila, I'm a dentist. However, it goes deeper than that. I love dentistry, but there's more about it that I don't love. So why do things you don't love? Life is short and I'm midway to my tombstone.

Why not change the things that I want to change? That's exactly what I'm doing. I wrote this book and several programs that will help so many more people than what I'm doing at the dental office.

In so doing, this will bring me mental and physical wealth that will replace my dental practice wealth, and when that happens, I will get out of dentistry. That's my main goal: to retire from dentistry so I can pursue my passion, which is writing and psychology. I want to have the time and energy to help people dive deeper into the reasons why we do the things we do.

That's my main mission, to make others understand themselves, and make them happy. Not from what I can do *for* them, but what *they* can do for themselves. If we all become masters of our own life history, we can write the story we are proud of!

Mastery of something has more to do with seeing things that no one else can see. You can predict the future because of the actions that are taken in the present. You can control the moment, so the moment is grasped, and not let go.

This doesn't mean that you have to be the best at everything. No one can. But true mastery is becoming aware of your true talents and abilities, your instincts about something, your general character, and develop them to their upmost potential.

No one knows what you're capable of, not even you. Don't you want to find out?

If you want to play a professional sport, and you have the ability and the talent, but you don't quite know the steps to making it happen, don't you think you should ask someone? Ask someone who has already done it. Then just do what they say to do. The odds are better if you do that than if you try to figure it out on your own, especially when you don't know how.

Everyone has to start from the beginning. I do all of the time. I've learned to check my ego at the door. I've learned to ask intelligent questions and ask a lot of "how to" questions so that I know what my steps are, and then I just do them.

I have trained myself not to question the "how to" steps, or think about *why* I need to do them. That is counterproductive. It wastes a lot of time, money, and thought power that I could be using to do the steps my mentor has laid out for me. Make it simple! I know that I can succeed if I don't get in my own way. Here's what you need to do, then just do it!

Mastery of one thing always leads to questions about something else in your life. That's what it's meant to do. It expands your awareness and pulls off the blinders that have been giving you the same results over and over again.

If you've mastered your management skills, your talents can then be used to own your own business, or start a consultation business on management, or even organizing your local softball league.

Mastery of a skill can affect big things or small things in your life. But the main point is that it can open you up to so much more. It can increase your experiences and your memories, and you'll be able to help so many more people with your skill set. How exciting is that?

I'm so pumped up right now!

As I'm writing this, I'm so eager to finish things up so that I can work on my programs that go with this book, and the ideas in it, so I can help more people get what they want. It's amazing to me how our imagination can take us to places we never knew we could go, physically and emotionally. It feels so wonderful! I'm proud and excited that I could share these thoughts with you.

I have been using the habit formula for years without being *aware* that I was doing it. I would just want something, find a mentor or trainer, and then just do what they told me. The older I get, you would think that you can't teach old dogs new tricks, but I've become more and more excited to learn different things in life.

I've opened up my mind to the new thoughts and possibilities that have come with creating this book. The people that I've met, their reactions to this book, and my thoughts on this subject have been nothing but remarkable and almost mind-blowing.

I want you to have the same experience in your life. I want you to be sick and tired of being sick and tired, get off your butt, and start living the way you want to live. If you want to live in a different place, find out how to do it, and get moving. If you want more money, find someone who is making more money than you, and follow their advice. If you want to find love, get out into the world, and meet people. There are so many people that want to find the same thing as you, but if you don't get out of your pajamas, you'll never meet them.

If you want to stop being negative, join a church or email me, I'm always upbeat, and can help you get your mind on the positive side. Remember, there's *always* someone worse off than you! You could be dead!

If you want to be more organized, find some articles or a YouTube video, or hire a professional organizer to come to your house and show you how to become organized.

If you want to have more freedom and time for your family, you need to learn how to say no, find ways of being more efficient and effective, and enjoy all the free moments you have with them.

But *you* must do it! I can't do it for you. I can be your mentor and cheerleader, but until you realize *what* you must change, decide that you're *going* to change, find someone to show you *how* to change, and then start *moving* in the direction of the change, nothing will happen! You won't become the master of your life until you make those changes!

I want to thank you taking your time to recognize your habits and learn how to effectively change the bad ones, so you can create the life you want. Find the strength to complete the assignments after all the chapters, and I can't wait to hear about the wonderful things you've accomplished by doing these tasks.

Join my Facebook page, and let me know how you're doing and what you've done with your life.

Go for it! You'll be so happy and proud of yourself of what you've accomplished!

Remember that you can do anything you set your mind to; you just have to take action to get the results!

For mentoring and private coaching, go to www.thehabitformula.com or my parent company www.powersourcemedia.net.

Assignment #7

A. What other areas of your life can you improve that you didn't list in any other chapter activities? List 5.

Example List:

1. Get out of work on time.
2. Learn to play the guitar.
3. Become a public speaker.
4. Learn Spanish.
5. Have Sunday family dinners.

B. List 5 things that are holding you back from making these changes:

Example List:

1. Too many things to do at work.
2. Time to practice the guitar.
3. Fear of being in front of a group.

4. No one to practice Spanish with.

5. Just don't plan it.

So, you see the repetition in this?

You already accomplished 5 things, now we're ready for the next 5 things. And the next ones, and the next ones.

We do it the same way every time. As long as you work on something every day, you will make those habits that will change your life forever and no goal will be too big to accomplish!

www.ingramcontent.com/pod-product-compliance
Lightning Source LLC
Chambersburg PA
CBHW021410290426
44108CB00010B/466